COCO CAKE LAND

COCO CAKE LAND

Cute and Pretty Party Cakes to Bake and Decorate

LYNDSAY SUNG

ROOST BOOKS
Boulder 2018

Roost Books
An imprint of Shambhala Publications, Inc.
4720 Walnut Street
Boulder, Colorado 80301
roostbooks.com

9 8 7 6 5 4 3 2 1

First Edition
Printed in China

⊛ This edition is printed on acid-free paper that meets
the American National Standards Institute Z39.48 Standard.
♻ Shambhala Publications makes every effort to print
on recycled paper. For more information please visit
www.shambhala.com.

Distributed in the United States by Penguin Random House
LLC and in Canada by Random House of Canada Ltd

Designed by Liz Quan

LIBRARY OF CONGRESS CATALOGING-IN-PUBLICATION DATA

Names: Sung, Lyndsay.
Title: Coco cake land: cute and pretty party cakes to bake and
decorate / Lyndsay Sung.
Description: First edition. | Boulder: Roost Books, 2018. |
Includes index.
Identifiers: LCCN 2017030185 | ISBN 9781611803150 (hard-
cover: alk. paper)
Subjects: LCSH: Cake. | Cake decorating. | LCGFT: Cookbooks.
Classification: LCC TX771 .S875 2018 | DDC 641.86/53—dc23
LC record available at https://lccn.loc.gov/2017030185

To my mom and dad,
for their guidance and support of their wildest daughter.

To my husband, Rich,
for being the calming factor and love of my life.

To my son, Teddy,
the sweetest and wildest of them all.

C●NTENTS

INTRODUCTION

Cake is kinda the best thing ever. So long as there's frosting, it is the one thing I'll practically never turn down, no matter how terrible. From supermarket sheet cakes to fancy layer cakes to Dairy Queen ice cream cakes with the fudgy crunch middle, I will have my fork ready any way you slice it.

There was a time when I was not known for being Ms. Coco Cake Land. In fact, the first cake I fully remember making was a hot mess (I've come a long way!). It was for my husband, Rich, who was my vegan boyfriend at the time. I made a vegan vanilla cake from scratch. There was a particular no-name-brand frosting at the grocery store that happened to be vegan, so I bought that, and a couple of squeeze-it tubes of blue icing to help me scrawl out "Happy Birthday Rich." To top off this beauty, I found some plastic deer and trees at the dollar store and plunked them into the oily, tooth-rottingly sweet frosting. I didn't know about leveling a cake, or crumb coating, or offset spatulas.

So it was a frosting-with-crumbs cake with a definite uneven peak in the center, blue icing serial-killer writing, and some probably not very food-safe toys stuck into it. But I did it. I had baked a cake from scratch, frosted it, and decorated it. It was awful looking, but I was proud.

Several years later I became obsessed with baking. I baked my way through *Martha Stewart's Baking Handbook* and tried making everything from macarons to pies to cupcakes to Swiss meringue buttercream to sandwich cookies. I started churning out cupcakes, and all of a sudden I had a weird little cottage-industry biz going out of my home kitchen. I documented all of the cupcakes and cakes I was making and started a blog to slap up my point-and-shoot digital photos, along with a few stories. It was my Very Hungry Caterpillar Cake that catapulted (caterpillar-ulted?) my blog out into the world. That post went viral, and more of my cakes and posts were shared.

I slowly upgraded my blog and worked hard at growing it, investing in a better camera and adding tutorials, recipes, and lots of stories. Over the years, my blog *Coco Cake Land* has become my main source of work—baking and photographing cakes, creating content for other sites, working with brands, and experimenting and having a blast in the kitchen. Of course it helps that I love what I do: writing, photography, and baking cakes. "Not too shabby," as my beloved late grandmother used to say.

When it comes to cake decorating, my main squeeze will always be buttercream piping. I adore a mix of modern and vintage applications, and have a deep, undying love for the piping bag and for anything and everything kawaii cute. My signature style has become a mix of piped buttercream animal cakes with fondant features; lots of crafty elements, such as hand-drawn cake flags; an affection for typography; and plenty of vibrant color.

My path to becoming a baker and cake decorator was not direct. I was lucky enough to be able to follow something I was excited about. I worked hard at it, and I continually learn new things about baking and cooking. I also love styling the food and the props; snapping the photos makes me oddly giddy with joy. I chuckle when people ask for my "expert opinion," because I think of myself as just some nut bar dinking around making cakes and photographing them on her kitchen table.

Sometimes people give up on baking because they're not nailing it on the first go. But if at first you don't succeed and your cake is rock hard and tastes like garbage, don't give up. It takes time to develop your baking and cake decorating skills. No baby was born knowing how to make a perfect piecrust. You have to learn that by feel, repetition, and growing intuition. Practice, make an ugly cake, then figure out your mistakes and make a better one. Keep tweaking it.

In this book you will find cakes that I have made with love. Included are my signature animal cake designs, along with simple and colorful cake ideas to seriously jazz up your next birthday, celebration, or party. Along with my favorite cake designs, I've also included my go-to cake and frosting recipes so you don't have to worry one iota about baking your cake, decorating it, and eating it too. Step into my funny little world—I can't wait to see what you're going to make!

ON CELEBRATIONS

Life is a pretty sweet fruit, guys. I know this firsthand, because in 2015 I was diagnosed with breast cancer, and here I am—still alive. At the time, my son was two, I had just signed this book deal, and my husband was about to graduate from medical school. We were trying to have another baby, life was just rolling along, and all of a sudden everything screeched to a deafening halt. I had surgery, chemo, radiation, and many rounds of another targeted IV treatment. I lost all my hair and went through periods of feeling gutted, depressed, scared. But my son's laugh, his energy, and my love for him powered me through, as did my husband's unending support and the love of my family and friends. I finished active treatment in the spring of 2016, and every day I try to take a moment to be mindful, to stop and appreciate something good, sweet, or funny.

A cake was never just a cake in my book, but after cancer a birthday cake has become an even more meaningful signifier: I get to see another year, I get to see my son, Teddy, grow older, and I get to be the person who makes him his special cake. Nothing beats the magical twinkle in the eyes of a child as a candle-lit cake is set before him or her, the sweet sound of the "Happy Birthday" song in the air. And for me, as that person who made the cake, it creates a feeling I cherish; it's like a giant buttercream-frosted hug. One day, pictures from Teddy's fourth birthday might resurface, with his orange tiger cake with rainbow layers, and perhaps he will realize a little more just how much he was adored.

Life is short. Enjoy the good times, treasure your loved ones, and don't forget to *eat cake*.

LET'S BAKE A CAKE!

BAKING AND DECORATING BASICS

This section is about rules, tools, and keeping your cool—I like to whisper to myself "Zen cupcake" when I'm about to lose my mind in the kitchen and need to center myself. We'll talk about baking tips, my favorite baking supplies, and how to level, fill, and frost your cakes, plus go over piping basics and how to work with fondant.

BAKING TIPS

Before you swan dive into your very first homemade birthday cake, I'm going to share with you some hot tips on how to bake a cake successfully—things I've learned over many years of cake-making hardship, failures, trials, and tribulations.

● Read through the entire recipe or tutorial first! That way you can have a visual in your mind of what the end goal is, instead of blindly scrambling along step by step.

● Start with room-temperature ingredients—everything melds better that way. Butter is crucially required to be at room temperature. You can bring fridge-cold butter to room temperature by roughly dicing up the whole block into small pieces and letting them sit out for a good hour.

● Preheat the oven. It stinks to have your cake batter all ready and then you realize you forgot to turn the oven on.

● Prep your cake pans. I use a gentle spritz of vegetable oil cooking spray on the entire surface of the cake pan, sides and all, and then add a layer of parchment paper cut to size. Then I even lightly spritz the top of the parchment paper, because I'm paranoid about the cake sticking. If you're anti–vegetable oil spritz, rub some butter all over the pans and lightly flour instead. Just do *something*, I'm begging you!

● Prep your ingredients. Pretend you're on a cooking show and measure out and place each ingredient in its own little bowl. Cute, right? This way, you'll never wonder if you forgot the baking powder or the salt.

● Pay close attention to your batter when mixing. The worst thing is overmixing your cake batter, which activates the gluten in the flour and causes the final cake to stiffen. We're looking for a gentle, tender crumb—not an oversized hockey puck. Depending on the method, I always mix my cake batter on low speed until just incorporated, about 30 to 60 seconds max.

● Fill each cake pan evenly with batter and smooth the batter with an offset spatula.

● Keep a close eye on your cakes once they are in the oven; overbaked cakes are sad, dry cakes. Start testing for doneness a few minutes before the suggested baking time. Your cake will be finished baking when a toothpick or cake tester inserted into it comes out clean and your cake is springy to the touch.

● I let my cakes cool in their pans, set on wire racks. If it's a cold day, I'll set them outside on my back porch to cool faster.

● If you've overbaked your cake a little, don't panic. Remove the cake from the pan, let it cool, level it, and then use a pastry brush to brush on some vanilla simple syrup (see page 85). This can help remoisten the cake layers; however, it does add sweetness.

Make sure your cake layers are completely cool before you begin frosting and decorating.

There is nothing sadder than buttercream melting into a still-too-warm cake. If you're in a rush, power chill your cake layers in the freezer for 20 to 30 minutes, until they are cool enough to frost.

BAKING AND DECORATING EQUIPMENT

Balloon Whisk. Use this tool for whisking together dry ingredients or gently bringing a ganache together.

Cake Bench Scraper. A bench scraper is the holy grail of smoothness! These come in varying sizes and materials—plastic, acrylic, or metal. I use a basic metal one most of the time.

Cake Boards. Decorating your cake on a cake board makes transporting your cake so much easier, and it gives you a decorative base upon which to present your creation. You can find cake boards online, at cake supply shops, or in craft superstores. You can also buy them in bulk online (see Resources, page 164). The sidebar on page 165 gives instructions on covering your cake board with craft paper for a custom look.

Cake Pans. I have cake pans in all the sizes, but my go-to size is a round 8 by 2-inch pan. Most of the cake recipes in this book call for that size.

Cake Turntable. Turntables make your life so much easier when frosting and piping a cake. This tool is worth the investment.

Candy Thermometer. A candy thermometer or a digital read thermometer will be your special friend for making Vanilla Swiss Meringue Buttercream and Swiss Meringue Kisses.

Circle Cutters. I often use a set of circle cookie cutters for a nice, cleanly finished

edge when cutting out fondant facial features, like animal cheeks.

Dry Measuring Cups and Spoons. Exactitude is pretty crucial in recreating baking recipes. Invest in a solid set of cups and spoons, and they will last a lifetime. I use a stainless steel set, and they're more than a decade old now!

Flower Nail. A few of the projects in this book use buttercream flowers. A flower nail is a tool that assists in making these. Essentially it looks like a nail with an oversized circular metal top. A 2-inch square of parchment paper is adhered to the nail via a dab of buttercream, and a buttercream rose is piped on top of the parchment paper, removed from the nail, and chilled in the freezer until firm, ready for use.

Liquid Measuring Cups. I have a few of these, and I'm always using them for measuring liquids, cracking eggs into, measuring batter, et cetera.

Nonstick Rolling Pin. Great for rolling out fondant for animal face details.

Offset Spatula. I have a bunch of offset spatulas in varying sizes. They are terrific for leveling cake batter in the pan before putting it into the oven and for spreading frosting.

Parchment Paper. Parchment paper has so many uses: cut it into circles to line cake pans, use it to line baking pans for cookies, cut it into squares to pipe buttercream roses onto. Parchment paper may very well be my best baking pal.

Piping Bags. I use clear, disposable piping bags, but I reuse them: simply wash with hot water and dish soap.

COLORING CAKE BATTER

Colorful cake layers add an element of surprise and can carry a design from the outside to the inside. I love slicing into a cake and discovering the magic of colored layers.

To create colorful layers of cake, divide the cake batter into three medium-size bowls. Add a drop of gel food coloring in the color of your choice to each bowl, then proceed to fold in the color using a spatula, mixing slowly but efficiently and being careful not to overmix the batter. Pour each batch of colored batter into a separate cake pan to bake.

HOW TO FILL AND FROST A THREE-LAYER CAKE TO THE CRUMB COAT STAGE

The crumb coat is the first coat of buttercream on any cake. It will trap in any pesky crumbs, preventing them from marring the final visual product. Once we do the first crumb coat, the cake is chilled to cement the crumbs in place, making it ready for that final smooth buttercream layer or piped layer.

You will need a serrated bread knife for best results. Have your buttercream ready and piping bag filled, if using one. Have a cake board or cake plate ready on which to build your cake and set it on a cake turntable, if using.

Begin by placing a dab of buttercream on the center of your cake board. Carefully remove your first cooled cake layer from your cake pan, peel off the parchment paper if it's stuck to the cake, and place the cake layer flat side down on the cake board.

Examine your cake layer at eye level to discern how much, if any, of the dome you

Piping Tips. The main piping tips I use for my cakes are open star tips and my beloved multi-opening tip. My most-used tips happen to be Wilton: Wilton 1M is a classic open star tip, great for a perfect cupcake swirl, drop stars, and borders. Wilton 234 is my ultimate favorite for piping fur. Wilton 4B is a French open star tip, which I use for rosettes, drop stars, and shell borders. Wilton and Ateco are popular brand choices that can be found both online and more readily in stores, but please note that piping tip numbers are not standard and each brand has their own system.

Rubber Spatulas. I use rubber spatulas in various sizes. They are indispensable for scraping mixing bowls and transporting buttercream.

Serrated Knife. When leveling, a nice-quality long serrated knife is the only knife that will do to trim through the tender crumb of your precious cake layers! Use a gentle sawing action.

need to cut off for a nice, even top surface. Using the serrated knife, carefully and slowly level your cake, gently shearing off any cake dome that may have puffed up. You can save the cake trimmings for snacks later.

Add a layer of buttercream by using either a piping bag or an offset spatula. If using a piping bag, fit it with a large, open circle tip, fill it with buttercream, and pipe an even, generous layer of frosting about ½ inch thick across the leveled cake surface. Or, with a rubber spatula, place a large and friendly amount of buttercream in the center of your cake layer, then use your offset spatula to spread the buttercream evenly to the outer edges.

For the next layer, I like to remove the cake layer from the pan (leaving on the parchment paper if you used it), flip the pan over, and place the cake flat side down on top of the pan. Level your second layer the same way you did the first. Then carefully and deftly lift the cake layer off the pan and place the layer leveled side down on top of the buttercream-covered first layer, pressing down gently but firmly so that it adheres to the frosting. Peel off the parchment paper. Pipe or spread the buttercream over the second layer, using the same amount you used for the first layer.

Level your final cake layer as described above, placing it cut side down on top of the buttercream, again pressing down to adhere.

Now, we start on the crumb coat! Add a generous amount of buttercream to the top of the cake. Using your offset spatula, begin spreading it out to the edges, down the sides of the cake, then all around the cake, scraping the buttercream off into a separate bowl as needed. (We want to keep the "crumby" buttercream separate from the "clean"

buttercream.) Now, place your cake bench scraper against the side of the cake and turn your cake turntable at the same time, smoothing out the buttercream all around the cake, creating an even layer of buttercream, about ¼ inch thick.

When you're finished you'll find you've created a "lip" of buttercream around the top edge of the cake. Scrape this lip inward as you smooth the top of the cake into an even layer of frosting about ¼ inch thick. If you're going to be piping animal fur or rosettes on top, don't get too caught up in making this layer perfect, as the piping will cover up any lumps or bumps. Once you've smoothed your crumb coat to your liking, place the cake in the fridge or freezer to power chill for 20 minutes, until firm. This will lock in the crumbs.

Covering your own cake board

I love personalizing cake boards with **heavy-duty craft paper** in stripes, bright colors, or patterns. It's a simple way to make a cake board extra cute, and it's very easy to do. Using a **pencil,** trace a cake board circle on the back side of your craft paper. Cut out the paper circle using a pair of sharp **scissors.** Apply a fine layer of **glue-stick adhesive** to the top of the cake board, then carefully place the craft paper on top, smoothing it with your hands to help it adhere.

HOW TO FROST A CAKE TO THE FINAL COAT STAGE

Once your cake is firmly chilled, it's time for the final coat, aka the "beauty coat," that smooth outer layer of buttercream. Remove the cake from the fridge or freezer and place a generous dollop of buttercream on top. Begin spreading the frosting over the top and sides of the cake with your offset spatula. Smooth the top and sides with your cake bench scraper until you are pleasantly satisfied with its appearance. You can spend quite a while on this if you're feeling very perfectionisty. But don't fret too much if your first go at it is less than smooth—practice makes perfect.

PIPING BASICS

Put it in your bag and pipe it—buttercream, that is! Piping is what really gives cakes a professional vibe; even a simple piped border can add a fancy pro-feel finish. Piping buttercream can also create the delicious illusion of flowers in bloom or the fun look of animal fur, fish scales, and bird feathers!

How to fill a piping bag

If you are using a disposable piping bag, snip the end off and fit the piping tip in, pulling it snug. I find it's a huge help to employ a large yogurt container or tall plastic deli container to hold my piping bag so that I can fill it. Place the piping bag in the container and open the bag, pulling its edges over the sides of the container to create a nice opening. Using a spatula, fill the bag with buttercream until it is about half to two-thirds full; don't fill it all the way, as that makes it difficult to control. Lift the bag out of the container, twist the open end closed, and squeeze the bag so the buttercream flows into the tip.

Holding a piping bag

For maximum control, use your dominant hand (the hand you write with) to both hold and squeeze the larger end of the piping bag, and use your other hand to guide the bag by holding it closer to the tip. Make sure you twist closed the open end of the piping bag so buttercream doesn't come spurting out of the top. Some bakers like to use an elastic band or a clip to secure the opening; I just twist it closed, but experiment to see what works best for you.

How to pipe fur

To create cute animal cakes, you can pipe both short and long fur. Fit your piping bag with a large multi-opening tip and fill it with the buttercream of your choice. Holding your piping bag at a 90-degree angle against the cake, squeeze out spurts of buttercream— short spurts for short hair, slightly longer spurts for longer hair.

How to pipe drop stars

Using a piping bag fitted with an open star tip, such as Wilton 1M, hold the piping bag at a 90-degree angle against the cake surface. Squeeze the piping bag with medium pressure. As a drop star forms, stop squeezing and pull upward to release.

How to pipe a shell border

Using a piping bag fitted with a multipronged open star tip—also known as a French open star tip—such as Wilton 4B, hold the piping bag with your dominant hand at a 45-degree angle to the cake's top edge. Squeeze the piping bag with medium pressure so that a ridged buttercream ball shape forms, then pull gently away, creating a tail. Pipe the

next shell on top of the tail, going all the way around the top edge of the cake to make a fancy shell border.

How to pipe feathers

Using a piping bag fitted with a leaf tip of any size, hold the piping bag with your dominant hand at a 45-degree angle against the cake. Squeeze the piping bag with medium pressure until a leaf shape forms, then pull away. Continue piping in rows to create the textured look of bird feathers, but don't worry too much about having everything perfectly in line, as the more organic feathery look is very cute and natural feeling.

How to pipe scales

Originally known as a "petal pattern," this technique makes great fish scales! You will want to have a few clean paper towels, a

small offset spatula, and a piping bag fitted with an open circle tip. Start by holding the piping bag at a 90-degree angle against the cake. Squeeze out a ball of buttercream and pull away. Now press the offset spatula into the center of the ball, then pull the buttercream, creating a tail or streak of frosting. Wipe the offset spatula clean, then pipe the next ball on top of the tail. Continue along in this way, creating a scale pattern. You can alternate colors of scales, too!

How to pipe rosettes

Rosettes are one of my go-to frosting decorations. They look pretty as a border, and I've found they make a very adorable buttercream curly dog fur. Fit your piping bag with a French open star tip. Hold the piping bag at a 90-degree angle against the cake. Visualize the placement of the center of the rosette. Start piping from that center outward, going in a counterclockwise motion in one rotation. Pull away, creating a little "tail." Pipe the next rosette so that it's nestled closely to the previous rosette, beginning on top of the tail, and continue piping in this fashion.

How to pipe buttercream roses

First we will make a tight center scroll for our rose using the petal tip, which has a teardrop shape. Holding the piping bag at a 45-degree angle to the flower nail with the wide end of the teardrop on the bottom, squeeze the piping bag; turn the flower nail at the same time to form the center of the rose. Next, begin piping the first layer of petals. Squeeze the piping bag as you are turning the flower nail and make a slight down-up-down arc for the petal. Pipe the next petal in the same way, overlapping slightly, then pipe a third petal,

so there are three petals around the center roll. Keep making layers of petals until you have reached the desired size for your rose. I like for mine to have three layers of petals. Carefully remove the parchment paper from the flower nail with the rose attached and place it on a baking sheet or flat plate. Repeat the process for however many roses you wish to make. Once done, freeze the plate, uncovered, for at least 20 minutes, until the roses are cold and firm to the touch.

You can store your buttercream roses in the freezer for up to 1 month. Place them in an airtight container so they don't absorb any weird freezer smells. I always pipe many extra buttercream roses to have on hand for future projects, too, so feel free to squirrel away a bunch of buttercream roses now!

How to pipe multiple colors

I love adding more dimension and playfulness to my cakes by piping frosting in multiple colors. Fit your piping bag with the tip of your choice. Carefully spoon three colors vertically side by side into the piping bag so all the colors flow out at the same time. To get things flowing, point the piping bag at a side plate or piece of parchment paper, then gently squeeze so the colors reach the tip and pipe out a burst of buttercream onto your plate or paper.

WORKING WITH FONDANT

Fondant is a thick, sugary, doughlike icing that can be rolled and shaped and is sold commercially. Sometimes it has gelatin in it, but there are vegan versions. Some fondants are drier in certain climates, but since we aren't covering entire cakes with fondant in

this book and are simply using it for facial features and other accents, this isn't of huge concern. Still, fondant must be stored properly to maintain its pliability and to prevent it from drying out.

Fondant can be found readily online in a myriad of colors in small, consumer-grade containers. I use the brand Satin Ice, which is vegan, and it works well for me. If stored properly, fondant can last for up to 6 months. Here are some tips for working with fondant:

● Wash and dry your hands completely before handling fondant.

● I always have cornstarch on hand, as a touch of it here and there can prevent the fondant from getting too sticky.

● I use a nonstick plastic rolling pin for rolling fondant, but a regular rolling pin dusted lightly with cornstarch will do just fine.

● Fondant gets very sticky when it comes in contact with water or any kind of moisture. This works great when you're adding things like whiskers to cheeks: using a tiny bit of water acts as a "glue" and adheres small pieces together as the water dries.

● Fondant "sweats" when it is refrigerated or when it is in contact for too long with moisture—including the moisture of buttercream. I place my fondant pieces on my cake as close to serving time as possible, to avoid any potential "sweaty" beading. If you need to, you can make all the fondant pieces the

Alternatives to fondant

There are lots of great alternatives to fondant, many of which can be found at your grocery store. Also, piping facial features with buttercream is always a great option.

- Marzipan can be colored and worked with in a similar manner as fondant.

- Round candies, like malt balls, or chocolates, such as pistoles (couverture chocolate circles), make excellent eyes.

- Black shoestring licorice can be used for whiskers, eyebrows, and mouths.

- Pink gummy candies can make great animal noses.

- Brightly colored fruit taffy (such as Airheads) or fruit roll-ups can make great tongues.

- You can easily make animal ears using heavy-duty craft paper, too! Simply cut out the ear shapes, adhere to wooden skewers, and insert into the cake. Be careful not to let the ears touch the buttercream, as the paper can soak up the butter and appear "greasy."

---

evening before and wrap each piece individually with plastic wrap, then store all the pieces in an airtight plastic container at room temperature, ready to be placed on the cake shortly before guests arrive.

● You can color your own fondant using gel food coloring. Remember, with gel color, a little goes a long way, so start with a tiny amount first. Wearing food-safe gloves, knead it into the fondant until incorporated. Add more gel color as desired; if your fondant starts to get too wet, a sprinkle of cornstarch will help. Note: I try to avoid coloring my own fondant red or black; I find it's worth purchasing these fondants precolored, as it takes a lot of gel food coloring to achieve the desired shade and vibrancy (not to mention it can get very messy!).

● When making fondant in various colors into shapes, start with the white fondant first, then work with the black fondant last, so no black fondant bits get stuck in the white fondant.

● Fondant dries out and can become as hard as a rock, making it unusable. Always keep your fondant sealed airtight and stored in a cool, dry place when not in use.

Making fondant ears

The ear-making method depends on the type of animal cake you're creating. I use the triangle shape for the cat and the dog cakes, an oval shape for bunnies, and a rounded shape for bears. For this example I'll make cat ears. You will need white and pink fondant and two wooden skewer pieces.

Form two 1½-inch balls from the white fondant. Flatten them slightly and then shape them with your fingers to make flat triangle shapes, about ½ inch thick.

Divide the pink fondant into two ½-inch balls, flatten them to ¼ inch, and form them into triangles for the pink inner ears. Attach the smaller pink inner ears to the larger white triangles with a tiny amount of water to adhere. Insert the wooden skewer pieces into the bottom of each ear. Place the skewers into the cake.

Making fondant eyes

The amount of fondant you use for eyes depends on how big or small you want them to be. I like to use black fondant for eyes, but if you're emulating a beloved pet, feel free to customize! I like to make medium-size eyes, which use balls about 1 inch in diameter. Form two equal-size balls, and press each ball down gently to flatten to about ¼-inch thickness. You can use a toothpick tip's worth of water to adhere tiny white fondant highlights to the eyes.

Making fondant mouths, noses, and whiskers

To make a fondant mouth I use a small amount of black fondant—a ⅛-inch ball rolled into a snakelike shape, then curved into a smile.

For whiskers, you can define the length and shape to your exact liking. I roll small pieces of black fondant into long, thin whiskers.

I often set my whiskers on fondant cheeks. Using a small amount of cornstarch as needed to prevent stickiness, roll out the white fondant to a ⅛-inch thickness. Using a circle cutter, punch out two circle shapes for the cheeks, then adhere your whiskers to the cheeks with a tiny amount of water.

I generally use a piece of pink or black fondant (the colors animal noses tend to be) about ⅛ inch in size to make the nose. Roll it into a ball, then flatten it slightly to a ¼-inch thickness with your fingers while gently pulling it into your preferred shape—a triangle nose with nostril indents or even just a simple oval, Hello Kitty style!

ADDING CRAFTS TO YOUR CAKES

I love how a few simple craft elements can really personalize and give your cake an extra-cute aesthetic finish. I'm a big fan of using letter stamps and letter stickers in clean, modern fonts and even handwriting on cake flags. I use my trusty circle punch to cut out pieces of craft paper for a professional, clean cut—though hand cutting works great, too! Silly crafty elements can lend extra flair to your cakes: for instance, attaching paper fries to a burger cake or a paper bone to a dog cake are cute ways to add a special message or just an extra visual. Throughout this book I've made suggestions for crafty additions to the cakes, and templates can be found at the back of the book as well. I use heavy-weight craft paper, as I find that regular computer printer paper tends to sag or curl.

TIPS FOR CAKE SUCCESS!

Baking in Advance. Any cake in this book can be baked in advance and stored unfrosted. Simply double wrap tightly in plastic wrap and freeze for up to 1 month.

A simple cake topper: horse ribbon

I love vintage horse ribbons and wanted to make a cake topper in homage to their inherent cuteness. Pair this with a simple, classic ruffly-bordered vanilla buttercream cake for a stylish dessert centerpiece.

To make the Horse Ribbon, punch a circle out of a piece of **heavy-weight craft paper** using a **large circle craft punch** (I use a 3½-inch punch). Using **letter stickers**, spell out your message, leaving enough space to add ruffling around the edges of the circle.

Pinch pieces of **tissue paper confetti or 1-inch squares of tissue paper** into a ruffly flower shape. Add a tiny amount of **clear glue** to the edge of the craft paper circle and adhere the tissue paper. Continue gluing tissue paper flowers all around the edge until the entire edge is ruffled.

Using **scissors**, cut two pieces of **ribbon** to 3 inches in length each; finish the ribbon by making a V-shaped cut on the bottom edges. Attach the ribbons with a tiny amount of clear glue. Secure a **wooden skewer** to the back with a piece of **washi tape** cut to size.

Frosting Goals. All of the cakes in this book can be frosted with either Simple Vanilla Buttercream (see page 149) or Vanilla Swiss Meringue Buttercream (see page 151). The Simple Vanilla Buttercream takes on gel color quite well—you can get very bright and vibrant shades with very little gel color. Vanilla Swiss Meringue Buttercream, on the other hand, tends to take color in a more muted and more "chill" way than the simple buttercream. Just something to keep in mind when you're choosing between recipes for various cake projects! Both Simple Vanilla Buttercream and Vanilla Swiss Meringue Buttercream will keep for up to 1 week in the fridge, well wrapped and covered. Either recipe can be frozen up to 1 month, thawed to room temperature, then rewhipped in the bowl of a stand mixer to bring it back to full volume.

Plan Your Crafts. Crafty finishes such as cake flags and paper additions can all be made in advance to save time!

Fondant Features. I recommend making the fondant pieces only 1 day in advance of decorating the cake, as fondant will dry out over time and take on a not-so-fresh appearance.

Cutting the Cake. Most of the cakes in this book are three-layer, 8-inch round cakes. I've found these cakes serve sixteen guests with medium-size triangular slices. You can also cut the cake "wedding caterer" style, which entails cutting into squares or rectangles instead of triangles and will yield even more slices. If you're worried about not having enough, baking up a few dozen cupcakes on the side never hurts! The recipes in this book all translate well to cupcakes.

TIP This adorable cake topper can be saved as a memento—simply use hot, soapy water to wash the wooden skewer where it came in contact with the cake and dry it with a towel. I've saved many cake toppers from family birthday parties and celebrations by simply removing the skewers altogether and stringing the toppers along a piece of baker's twine to form a decorative garland.

CUTE CAKES

BLUE BEAR CAKE

for the cake base

1 recipe cake of your choice
(pages 146–48)

Three 8 by 2-inch cake pans

for the cake decoration

1 recipe (about 4 to 5 cups) Simple
Vanilla Buttercream (page 149)

⅛ teaspoon gel food color in sky
blue (or any color of your choice)

2-inch ball of white fondant

3-inch ball of light blue fondant
(or other color to match the
buttercream)

1-inch ball of black fondant

tools

Piping bag fitted with a
multi-opening tip

Large circle cookie cutter
(80mm)

Wooden skewer cut into
2 equal pieces

Toothpick

I made this cake for my son Teddy's second birthday.
He had told me repeatedly in his high-pitched little voice
that he wanted a "blue bear bear cake" that year. So for
his party, we had a blue bear bear cake along with pizza
and ice cream on a sunny August day, hosting a whole
gaggle of toddlers. Of course I couldn't resist making a
cute craft paper garland of a blue bear, a slice of pizza,
and an ice cream cone. The garland now hangs in Teddy's
bedroom, a sweet reminder of a fun-filled day.

Note: If you wanted to make a classic brown bear, use the
Simple Chocolate Buttercream (page 150).

1. Prepare the cake. Bake the three layers of cake according to the recipe instructions. Tint the buttercream with the blue gel color. Level, fill, and frost your cake to the crumb coat stage (see page 4) with the blue buttercream.

2. Fill a piping bag fitted with a multi-opening tip with the remaining blue buttercream.

3. Pipe the fur. Starting at the bottom edge of the cake, hold the piping bag at a 90-degree angle against the cake and squeeze in short spurts to create frosting dots in a line from bottom to top. Continue piping lines all the way around the cake, nestling the lines closely together. Pipe the top of the cake in the same manner, working in circles from the outside to the center, until the entire cake is covered in fur.

4. Make the fondant features. Clean and dry your hands completely. Using a small amount of cornstarch to prevent stickiness, roll out the white fondant to a ⅛-inch thickness. With the circle cookie cutter, punch out a circle shape. Gently pull on the sides of the fondant circle to coax it into more of an oval shape. Place on a piece of parchment paper.

5. Divide the blue fondant into two 1½-inch balls. Now, gently flatten each ball to a ½-inch thickness to form round, thick ears. Insert a wooden skewer into the bottom of each ear and push it until it's almost at the end of the ear but before it pokes through the other side. Set aside on parchment paper.

6. Pull off two ¼-inch balls of black fondant. Form two round balls and flatten them gently. Set aside on parchment paper. Using another ¼-inch ball, form and flatten it into a more oblong nose shape; set aside. Divide the remaining fondant into two pieces and create two thin snakes by rolling each piece between clean, dry palms. This will be your bear's smiley face.

7. Place the white fondant muzzle on top of the cake, positioning it in the center bottom third. Press down gently into the buttercream to adhere. Using a toothpick tip as your paintbrush, apply a very small amount of water to the black fondant nose, then place on top of the white muzzle. Do the same with the black snake smiley pieces.

8. Add the eyes by placing them on the buttercream and pressing in lightly to adhere. Don't squish them down; simply press enough so they stick.

9. Finally, insert the fondant ears into the side of the cake. Looking down at the cake, insert the ears at the positions of 10 and 2 o'clock.

Paper party garland

Using the **templates** (page 158), cut the pieces for the pizza, bear, and ice cream cone out of **craft paper**. I used orangey yellow, brown, and red for the pizza; blue and white for the bear; and white and brown stripes for the ice cream cone. **Glue** the paper pieces together and use a black felt **marker** to draw the details on the bear. **Tape** the pieces to a length of white **baker's twine**.

CAT CAKE

for the cake base

1 recipe cake of your choice
(pages 146–48)

Three 8 by 2-inch round cake pans

for the cake decoration

1 recipe (about 4 to 5 cups) Simple
Vanilla Buttercream (page 149)

4-inch ball of white fondant

½-inch ball of pink fondant

2-inch ball of black fondant

tools

Piping bag fitted with a
multi-opening tip

Small to medium-size circle cutter
(50mm or 60mm round)

Wooden skewer cut into
2 equal pieces

Chopstick

This cat cake pushes all the right party animal buttons, and it can be customized any way you like. Does your kitty have orange fur and little white patches on his face? Pipe white buttercream patches first, then pipe the rest in orange buttercream. Feel like making a hot pink cat cake with colorful cake layers? Yes. Yes, you can.

1. Prepare the cake. Bake the three layers of cake according to the recipe instructions. Level, fill, and frost your cake to the crumb coat stage (see page 4) using the uncolored buttercream.

2. Fill a piping bag fitted with a multi-opening tip with the remaining buttercream.

3. Pipe the fur. Starting at the bottom edge of the cake, hold the piping bag at a 90-degree angle against the cake and squeeze in short spurts to create a line of frosting dots from bottom to top. Continue piping lines all the way around the cake, nesting the lines closely together, until the outside of the cake is covered in fur. Pipe the top of the cake in the same manner, working in circles from the outside to the center, until the entire cake is covered in fur.

4. Make the fondant features. Clean and dry your hands completely. Using a small amount of cornstarch as needed to prevent

stickiness, roll out the white fondant to a ⅛-inch thickness. Using the circle cutter, punch out two circle shapes for the cat cheeks and set aside. Pull off two tiny balls of white fondant to make eye highlights and set aside. Re-form the remaining white fondant into a ball, divide it into two equal balls, then flatten and shape them into ¼-inch-thick triangles for ears.

5. With the pink fondant, pull off a ⅛-inch piece to make the nose. Roll it into a ball, then flatten it slightly with your fingers while gently pulling it into an oblong shape. Set aside. Split the remaining pink fondant in two, roll each into a ball, then form a small triangle for the inner ear, pressing the pink on top of the white. Insert the wooden skewer pieces into the bottom of each ear.

6. Divide the black fondant in half, and then divide one piece in half again. Form these two smaller pieces into two equal balls for the eyes and adhere the tiny white fondant highlights with a tiny amount of water. Divide the other half of the black fondant into four pieces, rolling each into a long, thin, snakelike whisker.

7. Now let's put the face on the cake. Press the cheeks gently into the cake side, almost resting on the bottom edge. Add the nose by pressing it gently into the buttercream right above where the two cheek circles meet. Press the black eyes into the buttercream. Since we are working on the side of the cake, you will want to gently press each eye enough to adhere well.

8. To apply the whiskers, I use a chopstick. Dip the chopstick into a little bit of water,

paint a tiny amount of water onto the white cheek where you will add a whisker, then place the whisker on the cheek and hold it in place for 30 seconds. Then gently press the part that reaches past the cheek into the buttercream, until it sticks. Do the same with the remaining three whiskers, two for each cheek.

9. Finally, add the ears! Looking down at the top of the cake. Find the halfway mark. Place the ears just in front of the halfway mark, along the outside edge. To finish, pipe short

spurts of buttercream fur along the edges and backs of the ears.

TIP Before I press the facial fondant features in, I will usually hover them over the cake to visualize their placement. Sometimes I end up changing the size of the eyes or of the nose. Feel free to adapt the size of the facial features in whatever way you think works best for your cake!

TURQUOISE BUNNY CAKE

for the cake base

1 recipe cake of your choice
(pages 146–48)

Three 8 by 2-inch round cake pans

for the cake decoration

1 recipe (about 4 to 5 cups) Simple
Vanilla Buttercream (page 149)

¼ teaspoon gel food color in
turquoise (I use a mix of equal
amounts of sky blue and teal,
about ⅛ teaspoon each)

5-inch ball of white fondant

1-inch ball of pink fondant

2-inch ball of black fondant

tools

Piping bag fitted with a
multi-opening tip

Small to medium-size circle cutter
(50mm or 60mm)

Wooden skewer cut into
2 equal pieces

Chopstick

This bunny cake is an homage to the shredded coconut bunny cake my mom used to make us when we were kids. I wonder if this is where my animal cake obsession originates? The turquoise bunny was requested by my sweet niece Brookie on her fifth birthday, but your bunny can be any color you wish. Making this for Easter brunch? Classic white or even pastel pink would be a cute choice. Baking it for Halloween? Add extra eyes in varying sizes and sharp vampire teeth. You could even make the cutest chocolate brown bunny and add a few edible flowers on top for a "spring has sprung" vibe.

1. Prepare the cake. Bake the three layers of cake according to the recipe instructions. Tint the buttercream with the turquoise gel color. Level, fill, and frost your cake to the crumb coat stage (see page 4) using the turquoise buttercream.

2. Fill your piping bag fitted with the multi-opening tip with the remaining buttercream.

3. Pipe the fur. Starting at the bottom edge of the cake, hold the piping bag at a 90-degree angle against the cake and squeeze in short spurts to create frosting dots in a line from bottom to top. Continue piping lines all the way around the cake, nestling the lines closely together. Pipe the top of the cake in the same manner, working in circles from the outside to the center, until the entire cake is covered in fur.

4. Make the fondant features. Clean and dry your hands completely. Using a small amount of cornstarch to prevent stickiness, roll out the white fondant to a ⅛-inch thickness. With the small circle cutter, punch out two circle shapes for the bunny cheeks and set aside. Reserve two tiny balls to make eye highlights. Re-form the remaining fondant into a ball, then divide it in two.

5. Pull off a ⅛-inch piece of the pink fondant to make the nose. Roll it into a ball, then flatten slightly with your fingers while gently pulling it into an oblong shape.

6. With the remaining white and pink fondant, make two ears following the instructions on page 10; the pink fondant should be used for the inner ears. Shape them into bunny ears by making them oblong rather than pointed. Insert a wooden skewer piece into the bottom of each ear.

7. Divide the black fondant in half. Reserve one half for whisker making; divide the other half into two equal balls for the eyes. Make two eyes with white highlights following the instructions on page 11. Divide the remaining black fondant into four pieces, rolling each into long, thin snakes for whiskers.

8. Now let's put the face on the cake. Press the cheeks gently into the cake at the bottom edge of the cake side. Add the nose by pressing it gently into the buttercream. Press the black eyes into the buttercream. Since we are working on the side of the cake, gently press them in enough to adhere.

9. To apply the whiskers, Use a chopstick. Dip the chopstick into a little bit of water, paint a tiny amount of water onto the white cheek where you will add the whisker, then put the whisker in place, holding it there for 30 seconds. Then gently press the part of the whisker that reaches past the cheek into the buttercream to help it stick. Do the same with the remaining three whiskers, two for each cheek.

10. Finally, add the ears! Looking down at the top of the cake. Find the halfway mark and place the ears just in front of that mark, set apart from each other. Using your piping bag filled with buttercream, pipe short spurts of fur along the edges and backs of the fondant ears.

WHITE TERRIER DOG CAKE

for the cake base

1 recipe cake of your choice
(pages 146–48)

Three 8 by 2-inch cake pans

for the cake decoration

1 recipe (about 4 to 5 cups) Simple
Vanilla Buttercream (page 149)

3-inch ball of white fondant

¼-inch ball of pink fondant

2-inch ball of black fondant

tools

Piping bag fitted with a large
multi-opening tip

Wooden skewer cut into
2 equal pieces

The key to this pup is his moustache, in my humble opinion. Animals with hairdos and moustaches simply make me laugh—so this terrier pup's got quite the 'stache on him.

Either buttercream recipe will work wonderfully for this pup, tinted to match your dog if you like, or, try the Peanut Butter Frosting (page 156) or the Vegan Chocolate Whipped Ganache Frosting (page 153) if your doggy is on the brown-colored spectrum!

1. Prepare the cake. Bake the three layers of cake according to the recipe instructions. Level, fill, and frost your cake to the crumb coat stage (see page 4) using the buttercream.

2. Fill a piping bag fitted with a multi-opening tip with the remaining buttercream.

3. Pipe the fur. Starting at the bottom edge of the cake, hold the piping bag at a 90-degree angle against the cake and squeeze in short spurts to create frosting dots in a line from bottom to top. Continue piping lines all the way around the cake, nestling the lines closely together. Pipe the top of the cake in the same manner, working in circles from the outside to the center, until the entire cake is covered in fur.

4. Make the fondant features. Clean and dry your hands completely. Using a small amount of cornstarch to prevent stickiness, divide the white fondant ball in half. Make two ears

following the instructions on page 10. Insert the wooden skewer into the bottoms of each triangular ear. Looking down at the face, place the skewers into the side of the cake at approximately the 10 and 2 o'clock positions.

5. Flatten the pink fondant ball and gently pull it into an oblong shape. Using a paring knife, create an indentation down the center to make it look more tonguelike.

6. Divide the black fondant into three equal pieces; roll each piece into a ball. Make two eyes following the instructions on page 22. For the nose, flatten the third ball and work it into an oblong shape. Pinch the center bottom edge of the nose to create nostrils, indenting more pronounced nostril shapes to your liking.

7. Place the eyes on the cake and gently press them into the buttercream; do the same with the nose.

CRAFTY FINISHES

Woof cake flag

To make the cake topper, use a **3-inch circle punch** to punch out a 3-inch circle from the **craft paper**. (Alternatively, cut out the circle with **scissors**.) Adhere your cake message to the circle using **puffy alphabet stickers**. **Tape** the circle to a **wooden skewer** and insert it in the cake.

8. Using the piping bag, pipe long strands of fur starting at the top center of the cake and moving down to the eyes on each side to create bangs that look parted in the middle. Let the bangs cover parts of the eyes.

9. In the same way, pipe a moustache underneath the dog's nose—the bushier the better!

10. Tuck the pink fondant tongue underneath the piped moustache so it sticks up.

TIGER CAKE

for the cake base

1 recipe cake of your choice
(pages 146–48)

⅛ teaspoon gel food color in three
colors (optional)

Three 8 by 2-inch round cake pans

for the cake decoration

1 recipe (about 4 to 5 cups) Simple
Vanilla Buttercream (page 149)

¾ teaspoon gel food color
in orange

4-inch ball of white fondant

½-inch ball of pink fondant

3-inch ball of black fondant

tools

Piping bag fitted with a large
multi-opening tip

Medium-size circle cutter
(approximately 70mm)

Wooden skewer cut into
2 equal pieces

Chopstick

For my son Teddy's fourth birthday, I made this tiger cake (with turquoise, fuchsia, and yellow layers of cake) and a blue ghost piñata with a kawaii face. The mishmash theme reconfirmed for me that kids really don't care about a perfectly matched and designed birthday party—they just want to have fun, eat some cake, and rip open a few presents for good measure! I like to think you can throw a party that has some design elements but that still feels casual, heartfelt, and, most important, fun. I'm pretty sure my cute-animal-cake-making-for-Teddy days will soon be over ("Too babyish, Mom!"), but he dug into this cake happily.

1. Prepare the cake. Preheat the oven to 350°F. Make the cake batter according to the recipe instructions. Divide the batter evenly into three medium-size bowls. Add the gel food coloring of your choice to each bowl, then fold in the color using a spatula, mixing slowly but efficiently and being careful not to overmix the batter. Pour the batter into the prepared cake pans and use an offset spatula to level the batter. Bake according to recipe instructions. Let cool completely on wire racks.

2. Tint the buttercream with the orange gel color. Level, fill, and frost your cake to the crumb coat stage (see page 4) using the orange buttercream.

3. Fill a piping bag fitted with a multi-opening tip with the remaining buttercream.

4. Pipe the fur. Starting at the bottom edge of the cake, hold the piping bag at a 90-degree angle against the cake and squeeze in short spurts to create frosting dots in a line from bottom to top. Continue piping lines all the way around the cake, nestling the lines closely together. Pipe the top of the cake in the same manner, working in circles from the outside to the center, until the entire cake is covered in fur.

5. Make the fondant features. Clean and dry your hands completely. Using a small amount of cornstarch as needed to prevent stickiness, roll out the white fondant to a ⅛-inch thickness. Punch out two cheeks using the circle cutter. Pull off two tiny balls of fondant

for eye highlights and set aside. Form the remaining fondant into two balls; flatten them gently with your fingers to create thick, circular ears. Insert the skewers into the bottom center of the ears.

6. Divide the pink fondant in two equal pieces; roll the pieces into balls. Flatten the first ball with your finger, pulling it slightly to create an oblong tongue shape; using a paring knife, indent the center of the tongue. Form a nose by flattening the second ball slightly, pulling it gently into an oblong shape, then using your fingers to create indentations for nostrils.

7. Pull off two ½-inch pieces of black fondant. Make two eyes following the instructions on page 11. Roll out the remaining black fondant to a ⅛-inch thickness; using a paring knife, cut out six triangles about ¾ inch long each for the tiger markings. Cut a seventh triangle a bit larger for the widow's peak. Finally, roll out the eyebrows and four whiskers with the remaining black fondant.

8. Place the cheeks on the top of the cake and press them lightly into the buttercream to adhere. Add the pink nose and the tongue, again pressing them lightly to adhere.

9. Using a chopstick as a paintbrush, gently add a tiny line of water to the cheeks where you want a whisker to be; place the whisker there and hold for 30 seconds to adhere. Then press the other half of the whisker into the buttercream until it sticks. Repeat until you have attached all the whiskers.

10. Adhere the white fondant highlights to the black eyes with a tiny amount of water. Press the eyes gently into the buttercream. Add the eyebrows above the eyes.

11. Finally, add the tiger markings: two triangles on either cheek, with the points facing inward, and three on the top of the head, with the larger widow's peak in the center.

12. Place the white ears into the side of the cake at approximately the 10 and 2 o'clock positions.

PANDA CAKE

for the cake base

1 recipe cake of your choice
(pages 146–48)

Three 8 by 2-inch round cake pans

for the cake decoration

1 recipe (about 4 to 5 cups) Simple
Vanilla Buttercream (page 149)

3-inch ball of white fondant

4-inch ball of black fondant

tools

Piping bag fitted with a
multi-opening tip

Medium-size circle cutter (60mm)

Wooden skewer cut into
2 equal pieces

This Panda Cake is an homage to my Asian heritage: whenever I'm asked what my spirit animal is, pandas are always my go-to, simply because they are from China. Secretly, perhaps I'm actually a slightly Goth sea otter. This panda is so cute and easy to make. I like to think he has just come across a never-ending field of bamboo, reeds whistling in the warm air, hence his very high excitement level and sweet little smile.

1. Prepare the cake. Bake the three layers of cake according to the recipe instructions. Level, fill, and frost your cake to the crumb coat stage (page 4) with the buttercream.

2. Fill a piping bag fitted with a multi-opening tip with the remaining buttercream.

3. Pipe the fur. Starting at the bottom edge of the cake, hold the piping bag at a 90-degree angle against the cake and squeeze in short spurts to create frosting dots in a line from bottom to top. Continue piping lines all the way around the cake, nestling the lines closely together. Pipe the top of the cake in the same manner, working in circles from the outside to the center, until the entire cake is covered in fur.

4. Make the fondant features. Clean and dry your hands completely. Using a small amount of cornstarch to prevent stickiness, roll out the white fondant to a ⅛-inch thickness. Punch out two cheeks using the circle cutter. Shape white pupils by rolling two small balls and flattening them slightly.

5. Roll out the black fondant to a ⅛-inch thickness. Punch out two large black circles using the circle cutter and gently pull the shapes into ovals. Roll a piece of fondant into a ¼-inch ball, then gently pull it into an oblong shape for a small nose. Roll a small amount of fondant between your hands to make a long, thin mouth and a philtrum (the line that connects the nose and mouth).

6. Divide the remaining black fondant into two equal pieces. Roll each piece into a ball and flatten gently to make thick, circular ears. Insert a wooden skewer into each ear. Looking down at the face, slide the skewered ears into the sides of the panda cake; position them so they are slightly wider than 10 and 2 o'clock.

7. Adhere the white fondant pupils to the black eye ovals using a small amount of water. Gently press each eye into the top of the cake, placing them wide apart and angling them so the ovals point upward and toward the center.

8. Press both white cheeks into the cake. Using a tiny amount of water or buttercream, attach the nose, philtrum, and mouth.

HAPPY BIRD CAKE

for the cake base

1 recipe cake of your choice
(pages 146–48)

Two 6-inch round cake pans

One half–sports ball cake pan

Baking sheet (any size)

for the cake decoration

1 recipe (about 4 to 5 cups) Simple
Vanilla Buttercream (page 149)

¼ teaspoon gel food color in teal

¼ teaspoon gel food color in
sky blue

3-inch ball of blue fondant

½-inch ball of yellow or
orange fondant

1-inch ball of black fondant

tools

Bubble tea straw or wooden skewer
for doweling the cake (optional)

Piping bag fitted with a
large leaf tip

I love this cute little chirpy fella, whom I've dolled up in blue buttercream feathers. The piped feather effect is thanks to the handy-dandy leaf tip. Using a sports ball cake pan gives this cake a 3-D look, without the muss, fuss, and scariness of having to carve a cake. Mr. Happy Bird's feathers can be piped in any color you like, even in rows of rainbow colors if you're feeling fancy.

1. Prepare the cake. Preheat the oven to 350°F. Make the cake batter according to the recipe instructions. Arrange the sports ball pan so it sits on its metal ring and place on a baking sheet. Fill the sports ball pan about two-thirds full with batter. Divide the rest of the batter between the two 6-inch pans. Use an offset spatula to level the batter. Bake according to recipe instructions; the sports ball pan will take longer to bake, about 25 minutes. Start checking doneness for the 6-inch layers after around 15 minutes, removing from the oven when a toothpick inserted in the center comes out clean. Continue baking the sports ball layer until it is done and remove from the oven. Let the layers cool completely on wire racks.

2. Tint the vanilla buttercream with a mixture of teal and blue gel food colors. Level, fill, and frost your cake to the crumb coat stage (see page 4) with the buttercream; the top will be the sports ball layer. (Optional: To give the cake some sturdiness for frosting, insert a bubble tea straw or wooden skewer cut to size through the center of the three layers.) Chill the crumb-coated cake in the fridge or freezer for 30 minutes.

3. Fill the piping bag fitted with a large leaf tip with the remaining blue buttercream.

4. Pipe the feathers. Get ready to pipe some feathers, y'all! Starting at the bottom edge of the cake, hold the piping bag at a 90-degree angle against the cake and squeeze, pulling a triangular feathery shape in a line from bottom to top. I like to make some feathers longer and some shorter to give Happy Bird's plumes an organic feel. Continue piping lines all the way around the cake, nestling the lines closely together, until the entire cake is covered. The nice thing about the feathers is if you have a weird little bald patch somewhere or if you think your piped lines aren't lining up, you needn't fret—you can pipe in more feathers anywhere you like, and the overall effect is of a cute, feathery bird.

5. Make the fondant features. Clean and dry your hands completely. Divide the blue fondant into two pieces. Roll each piece into a thick log, about 2 inches long. Gently flatten each log to a ½-inch thickness, while also forming one end to a point for the wing. While the fondant is still pliable, apply one wing to the side of your bird; gently curve the wing so the tip will sit flat on the cake board, helping to hold up the weight of the fondant. Gently press the rest of the wing into the buttercream to adhere. Do the same to the other side.

6. Form the yellow or orange fondant into a flat, thick, triangular beak, about ¼ inch thick and about the size of a penny. Stick the beak into the buttercream.

7. Divide the black fondant into two pieces. Roll each piece into a thick snake and then curve them slightly to create happy closed eyes! Place them on the cake. (Alternatively, you can make open eyes using white and black fondant; see page 11).

TIP Sometimes when I'm piping this bird, my lines veer off to the side, and it looks uneven as I'm going along. But because the shape of the feathers vary—some stick down, some up, some are longer, and some are shorter—the overall effect is very feathery. You can remove any mistakes with the tip of a knife and pipe another feather on top.

PINK LAMB CAKE

for the cake base

1 recipe cake of your choice
(pages 146–48)

Three 8 by 2-inch round cake pans

for the cake decoration

1 recipe (about 4 to 5 cups) Simple
Vanilla Buttercream (page 149)

½ teaspoon gel food color in pink

3-inch ball of white fondant

1-inch ball of pink fondant

1-inch ball of black fondant

tools

Piping bag fitted with a French
open star tip

Wooden skewer cut in
2 equal pieces

This Pink Lamb Cake was inspired by my niece's pink lamb security blanket with a sleepy-cute face. I made this for her second birthday, and I love the use of rosettes for that tight-perm lamb's hair feel. You can do a sleepy face or open eyes—either way, this cake is as curly and cute as can be.

1. Prepare the cake. Bake the three layers of cake according to the recipe instructions. Tint the vanilla buttercream with the pink gel food color. Level, fill, and frost your cake to the crumb coat stage (see page 4) with the pink buttercream. Chill it completely in the fridge or freezer for approximately 20 minutes until firm, then frost only the top of the cake with the final coat (see page 6). Make it as smooth as you can, to create a nice, flat surface for your lamb's face. Chill the cake again for 30 minutes, until the buttercream sets.

2. Fill a piping bag fitted with the French open star tip with the remaining pink buttercream.

3. Pipe the curly fur. Starting from the bottom edge of the cake, hold the piping bag at a 90-degree angle against the cake. Pipe your first rosette (see page 8). Pipe the next rosette on top of the "tail" of the first one. Continue piping, creating a line of rosettes all the way around the base of the cake.

4. Begin your next row of rosettes and pipe all the way around the cake. Continue piping the rosette rows until you reach the top of the cake. Now, pipe on a row of rosettes around the top edge of the cake, connecting your rosettes from the sides with the top. Looking down at the top of the cake, imagine where the face will go. Pipe a few swirls of curly pink fur like a widow's peak for your lamb.

5. Make the fondant features. Clean and dry your hands completely. Using the white fondant and half of the pink fondant, make two ears following the instructions on page 10. Insert a wooden skewer into the bottom of each ear.

6. Use the remaining pink fondant to form the nose. Roll the fondant into a ball, then flatten and form into a triangle with a rounded top. Using your fingers, add little indents for nostrils.

7. Divide the black fondant into four equal pieces. Roll them into skinny snake shapes—two for closed, sleepy eyes and two for the smile.

8. Gently press the sleepy eyes into the buttercream to adhere; do the same with the pink nose and black smile.

9. Add a few more rosettes to the widow's peak hairdo if needed, varying them in size if you like.

10. Now, gently push the ear skewers into the sides of the cake. I like the floppy-eared look, which works best just below the 10 and 2 o'clock positions.

TIP If you muck up any of the components of this lamb cake, don't fret! I've had many instances of too-soft buttercream that makes an undefined rosette. Simply remove the offending rosette with an offset spatula, chill the buttercream in its piping bag in the fridge for a few minutes, and pipe right over where the old rosette was. If you don't like the size or shape of the fondant nose you made, remove it and try again!

ORANGE FOX CAKE

for the cake base

1 recipe cake of your choice
(pages 146–48)

Three 8 by 2-inch round cake pans

for the cake decoration

1 recipe (about 4 to 5 cups) Simple
Vanilla Buttercream (page 149)

1 teaspoon gel food color in orange

5-inch ball of black fondant

Small amount of white fondant

tools

Piping bag fitted with a
multi-opening tip

Wooden skewer cut in
2 equal pieces

This cake design was inspired by my son Teddy's orange fox decal in his bedroom, a cute, simple, friendly fox ready to party it up! It's an easy-breezy cake for the beginner cake decorator and would work well for a woodland-themed party.

1. Prepare the cake. Bake the three layers of cake according to the recipe instructions. Level, fill, and frost your cake to the final coat stage (see page 6) using the vanilla buttercream. Make the top of the cake as smooth as possible.

2. Tint the remaining buttercream with the orange gel color.

3. Fill a piping bag fitted with a multi-opening tip with the orange buttercream.

4. Pipe the fur. Starting at the bottom edge of the cake, hold the piping bag at a 90-degree angle against the cake and squeeze in short spurts to create frosting dots in a line from bottom to top. Continue piping lines all the way around the cake, nestling the lines closely together, until the entire sides are covered in fur.

5. Now, looking down at the top of the cake, pipe two curved lines of fur that meet in the middle. If you wish, you can use a toothpick to lightly draw the two curved lines in the buttercream as a guide first. Then pipe on top of the lines. Fill in the top part of the cake with more piped fur; fill in the center line as well, leaving the cheeks white.

6. Make the fondant features. Using a 2-inch ball of the black fondant and the small amount of white fondant, make two eyes with highlights following the instructions on page 11.

7. Pinch off a small amount of the black fondant to form two little eyebrows. Make the nose with a ½-inch piece of black fondant by rolling it into a ball, then squishing it down slightly and indenting with two fingers to create nostrils.

8. With the remaining black fondant, make black ears following the instructions on page 10. Insert the wooden skewer pieces into the bottom of each ear and, looking down on the face, insert them into the side of the cake at about the 10 and 2 o'clock positions.

9. Place the face on top of the cake. Set the eyes into the white buttercream and gently press to adhere. Position the eyebrows in the orange buttercream just above the eyes. Finally, place the nose on the bottom of the fox's face, pressing gently into the buttercream to adhere.

BROWN CURLY-HAIRED PUP CAKE

for the cake base

1 recipe cake of your choice
(pages 146–48)

Three 8 by 2-inch round cake pans

for the cake decoration

1 recipe (about 4 to 5 cups)
Simple Chocolate Buttercream
(page 150)

2-inch ball of white fondant

½ inch ball of pink fondant

3-inch ball of brown fondant (to
match the buttercream)

2-inch ball of black fondant

tools

Piping bag fitted with a French
open star tip

Medium to large circle cookie cutter
(60mm to 70mm)

Wooden skewer cut into
2 equal pieces

Edible marker in black (such as
AmeriColor Gourmet Writer; see
Resources, page 164)

Who doesn't love a dog with a perm? Or dreadlocks, for that matter? I'm all about the dogs with hair-styles. This brown pup has cute curly buttercream fur, courtesy of one of my favorite piping techniques—the buttercream rosette! Master the rosette, and you're on your way to many curly-haired, furry-faced cakes in your future.

1. Prepare the cake. Bake the three layers of cake according to the recipe instructions. Level, fill, and frost your cake to the crumb coat stage (see page 4) with the Simple Chocolate Buttercream. Chill the cake in the fridge or freezer for 20 minutes to set the buttercream.

2. Frost the top of the cake only with a second coat of buttercream, smoothing as best you can to create a nice, flat surface for your pup's face. Chill the cake again for 20 minutes to set the buttercream.

3. Pipe the curly fur. Starting from the bottom edge of your cake, hold the piping bag at a 90-degree angle against the cake. Pipe your first rosette (see page 8). Pipe the next rosette on top of the tail of the first one. Continue along, creating a line of rosettes all the way around the cake.

4. Begin your next row of rosettes and pipe all the way around the cake. Continue piping the rosette rows until you reach the top of the cake.

5. Make the fondant features. Clean and dry your hands completely. Using a little bit of cornstarch to prevent stickiness, roll out the white fondant to about a ⅛-inch thickness. Punch out two white cheeks with the circle cookie cutter.

6. Roll the pink fondant into a ball; flatten gently with your fingers and pull slightly to create a thick, flat, oblong shape for the tongue. Using a small knife, carefully indent the center (don't cut through the tongue!).

7. Divide the brown fondant into two pieces for the ears. Roll each piece into a ball. Gently flatten one and curve the fondant so it resembles a thick, rounded U shape. Insert a wooden skewer into one end of the U shape. Repeat with the other ball and wooden skewer.

8. Reserve a small portion of black fondant for the eyebrows and a ½-inch ball for the nose. With the rest of the black fondant, create two eyes with white highlights following the instructions on page 11. Create a nose following the instructions on page 11. Finally, roll out two thick snakes for eyebrows.

9. Hold the black edible marker upright at a 90-degree angle above the white fondant circles. Pressing the marker directly into the fondant, create a freckle. Make three freckles on each circle (or however many you wish).

10. Place the fondant features on top of the chilled cake, keeping in mind that you will do a final piping of curly hair on top afterward. Place the eyes at about 10 and 2 o'clock; press lightly to adhere them to the buttercream. Add the eyebrows in a rainbow shape to maintain the pup's happy demeanor. Add the white cheeks, then use a dab of buttercream to attach the nose on top. Nestle the tongue in between the cheeks, pressing in lightly to adhere it to the buttercream underneath.

11. Next, pick up your piping bag once again and begin piping a circle of rosettes at the very edge of the top of the cake. Pipe a "curly widow's peak" of hair onto the pup's face, with curly buttercream tendrils coming down between the pup's eyes.

12. Now, gently push the ear skewers into the sides of the cake. I like the floppy-eared look, which works best just below the 10 and 2 o'clock positions.

TIP If you aren't planning to serve the cake within a few hours of decorating it and you are in a warm or humid climate, note that the fondant might get a touch sweaty and shiny looking. You can always frost and pipe the cake the night before, store in the fridge (preferably wrapped up to avoid absorbing any fridge smells!), and bring it out once you're ready to set the fondant pieces in place and do the final curly-haired piping.

CRAFTY FINISHES

Happy birthday bone

Using the **bone template** (page 60) and a pair of **scissors,** cut a bone shape from a piece of **white craft paper.** Using a **marker,** write, "Happy Birthday" (or the message of your choice). **Tape the paper bone to a wooden skewer** and insert it into the cake.

RAINBOW UNICORN CAKE

for the cake base

1 recipe cake of your choice
(pages 146–48)

Three 8 by 2-inch round cake pans

for the cake decoration

1½ recipes (about 7 to 8 cups)
Simple Vanilla Buttercream
(page 149) or 1¼ recipes (about
8 cups) Vanilla Swiss Meringue
Buttercream (page 151)

⅛ teaspoon gel food color in green

⅛ teaspoon gel food color in pink

⅛ teaspoon gel food color in
sky blue

6-inch ball of white fondant

2-inch ball of pink fondant

2-inch ball of black fondant

tools

1 piping bag fitted with a
multi-opening tip

1 piping bag fitted with a
small leaf tip

2 piping bags each fitted with
open star tips

Wooden skewer cut into 2 equal
pieces, plus additional wooden
skewer (cut to fit, if need be)

Toothpick

While unicorns and rainbows share the same princessy territory that I normally avoid, I am not immune to their glory and delight. This cake represents unicorns in all their wonderment with rainbow curls, a pink twisty horn, and a happy little smile. If any cake called for colorful cake layers, this one would be it.

1. Prepare the cake. Bake the three layers of cake according to the recipe instructions. Level, fill, and frost your cake to the crumb coat stage (see page 4) using the uncolored buttercream.

2. Fill a piping bag fitted with a multi-opening tip with about half of the uncolored buttercream.

3. Pipe the fur. Starting at the bottom edge of the cake, hold the piping bag at a 90-degree angle against the cake and squeeze in short spurts to create a line of frosting dots from bottom to top. Continue piping lines all the way around the cake, nestling the lines closely together. Pipe the top of the cake in the same manner until the entire exterior is covered in fur.

4. Place ½ cup of the remaining buttercream into a medium-size bowl and tint it green. Fill the leaf-tipped piping bag with this buttercream.

5. Divide the rest of the buttercream evenly between two medium-size bowls, tinting one pink and the other, blue. Fill one of the star-tipped piping bags with the pink buttercream and the other with the blue.

6. Make the fondant features. Clean and dry your hands completely. First make the ears. Pull off two 1½-inch balls of white fondant; shape them into triangles about ½ inch thick. Using a 1-inch ball of pink fondant, form two flat triangles for the inner ears. Adhere these to the white triangles with a tiny amount of water. Insert wooden skewers into the bottoms of the ears and set aside.

7. To make the unicorn horn, pull apart 1½ inches of white fondant and roll it into a thick snake about 4 inches long. Do the same with the remaining pink fondant. Twist the white and pink fondant together, then roll the twist between your hands to compress it. Shape the tip of the horn into a point, then insert the additional skewer through the bottom center of the horn.

8. Reserve two tiny bits of white fondant for the eye highlights. To make the snout, use the remaining white fondant and roll out a

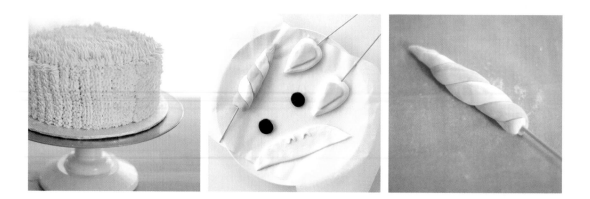

TIP For an extra flowery feel, add a few edible flower petals or whole organic flowers, such as roses or carnations. This is also a great time to use any extra buttercream roses you might have stored in your freezer.

half circle 6½ inches wide by 1½ inches high by about ⅛ inch thick. Using a sharp paring knife or pizza roller, trim to shape. With the trimmings, make three ½-inch-long U shapes; attach to the half circle with a tiny amount of water to make two nostrils and a smile.

9. Divide the black fondant into two equal balls, flattening them gently with your fingers to make ⅛-inch-thick circles. Use the two bits of reserved white fondant to create two tiny dots. Adhere the dots onto the black eyes using a toothpick and a teensy amount of water.

10. Place the ears and horn on the top of the cake. Place the eyes and snout on the front of the cake. Gently press all the pieces into the buttercream.

11. Using your two piping bags fitted with the open star tips and filled with colored buttercream, begin piping rosettes and drop stars on the unicorn head, alternating colors as you see fit and adding a cascade of swirls and drop stars to the center front, like a tendril of hair. Continue the curls and swirls all the way down the back of the unicorn's head—create a power mane full of magic! Finish by adding piped leaves using the piping bag fitted with the leaf tip for more texture and color.

FISH CAKE

for the cake base

1 recipe cake of your choice
(pages 146–48)

Three 8 by 2-inch round cake pans

for the cake decoration

1 recipe (about 4 to 5 cups)
Simple Vanilla Buttercream
(see page 149)

1 teaspoon gel food color in green

1 teaspoon gel food color in
sky blue or teal

½-inch ball of white fondant

Small amount of black fondant

2-inch ball of blue fondant

tools

2 piping bags, each fitted with
an open circle tip

Offset spatula

2 wooden skewers trimmed into
three 3-inch pieces (there will
be a leftover piece,
save for another use)

I sure do love this cute little fishy feller, piped with buttercream using the "petal technique." This cake works delightfully well for an undersea-themed children's birthday party or for that marine life or fishing enthusiast in your life.

1. Prepare the cake. Bake the three layers of cake according to the recipe instructions.

2. Place two-thirds of the buttercream into a medium-size bowl and mix in the green gel color. Place the remaining buttercream into a smaller bowl and mix in the blue gel color.

3. Level, fill, and frost your cake to the crumb coat stage (see page 4) with the green buttercream.

4. Chill your cake in the fridge or freezer for 20 minutes to set the crumb coat. Remove from the fridge and apply a final coat of green buttercream, using a cake bench scraper to smooth.

5. Fill one piping bag fitted with an open circle tip with the remaining green buttercream; fill the second piping bag with the blue buttercream.

6. Pipe the scales. Starting at the bottom edge of the cake, pipe alternating blobs of green and blue buttercream in a line from bottom to top. Using your offset spatula, drag each blob of buttercream along the side of the cake, creating a smear. Pipe a second row of buttercream just above the row of smears, again alternating colors. Perform the same pulling/dragging technique for each blob. Pipe and pull all the way around the cake sides to create the look of fish scales.

7. Once you are finished creating scales for the sides of the cake, let's work on the top! Looking down at your cake, begin piping blobs of buttercream at the far left edge of the top of the cake, following the rounded edge of the cake and again alternating colors. Using your offset spatula, drag each blob of buttercream to form scales, then pipe the next row. Continue until you have covered two-thirds of the cake top.

8. Make the fondant features. Clean and dry your hands completely. Reserve a tiny amount of white fondant for the eye highlight. Roll the rest of the white fondant into a ball and gently squish it down into a flat, thick circle. Using the black fondant and the white highlight, create an eye following the instructions on page 11.

9. Divide the blue fondant evenly into four pieces and hand-shape them into two triangles for fins, a tail, and fish lips. Curve the top of one fin slightly. I used a paring knife to create lines in the fins and tail. Insert a piece of wooden skewer into the base of the curved fin, the tail, and the lips. Looking down at the cake, insert the fin just behind the 12 o'clock position. Insert the lips in the 3 o'clock position and the tail in the 9 o'clock position. Looking down at the top of the cake, place the final fin in the center, gently pressing it into the buttercream. Place the eye on the right side, which you left free of scales.

TIP This method of making scales with buttercream can take a bit of time. Put on your favorite music and get into the Zen of repetitive motion for a while!

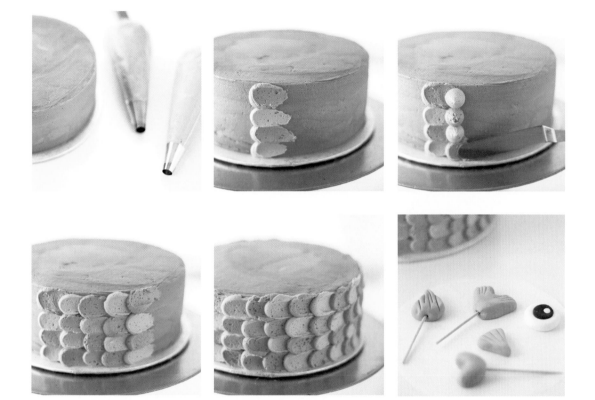

VINTAGE SAILBOAT CAKE

for the cake base

1 recipe cake of your choice (pages 146–48)

Three 8 by 2-inch round cake pans

for the cake decoration

1½ recipes (about 7 to 8 cups) Simple Vanilla Buttercream (page 149) or 1 recipe (6 cups) Vanilla Swiss Meringue Buttercream (page 151)

½ teaspoon gel food color in sky blue (more if using Vanilla Swiss Meringue Buttercream)

tools

Piping bag fitted with a French open star tip

This vintage-sailing-themed cake would be very cute for any sailor-type folks, like my husband, but also for a little sailor's first birthday party or a going-away party—bon voyage! The oceany buttercream look is achieved by using a French open star tip and creating rosette-type swirls in whatever pattern tickles your fancy. The simplicity of the cake toppers in the striped pattern give it the "vintage sailboat" feel. You could also swap out the boat-themed cake toppers for little paper-flag fishies and various sea creatures and serve it for an under-the-sea party.

1. Prepare the cake. Bake the three layers of cake according to the recipe instructions. Tint the buttercream with the blue gel color. Level, frost, and fill your cake to the crumb coat stage (see page 4) using the colored buttercream.

2. Pipe the ocean waves. Fill a piping bag fitted with the French open star tip with the buttercream. Starting at the bottom edge of the cake, hold the piping bag at a 90-degree angle against the cake. Squeeze the piping bag while moving in a counterclockwise circular motion, creating a series of rosettes— or, in this case, cascades of waves. Continue piping rosettes in rows all around the cake until you reach the top edge, about three or four rows.

3. On the top of the cake, continue piping rosettes but begin piping in a more free-form manner to mimic the idea of waves forming. Create some smaller and some larger rosettes, clockwise and counterclockwise rosettes, until you are happy with the organic oceanic feel of the cake.

CRAFTY FINISHES

Sailboat and moon

Using a **2-inch circle punch,** punch out a moon from a piece of **yellow craft paper. Tape** it to a **wooden skewer.** Punch out another circle from a piece of **striped craft paper.** Use **alphabet stamps** to create a cake message on the striped circle. Once the ink has dried, tape it to a wooden skewer. Using **scissors** and more striped craft paper, cut out a half circle and a right-angled triangle (see the **template** on page 161). Tape both to a wooden skewer to make a boat. Place the skewers in the cake at varying heights for visual interest.

CACTUS GUY CAKE

"Hidey ho, cacti!" This stumpy little cactus will be the life of your next party. No prickles on this character, just piped lines of buttercream and a loveable kawaii face. He's a fun little rascal for a Western-themed or Joshua Tree hippie party. Or make him to celebrate that lover of succulents in your life.

for the cake base

1 recipe cake of your choice
(pages 146–48)

Two 6-inch round cake pans

One half–sports ball cake pan

for the cake decoration

1 recipe (about 4 to 5 cups) Simple
Vanilla Buttercream (page 149)

½ teaspoon gel food color in green
(I use ¼ teaspoon kelly green
mixed with ¼ teaspoon
juniper green)

¼ teaspoon gel food color in red
(or color of your choice)

4-inch ball of white
(or green) fondant

White sugar pearls
(see Resources, page 164)

2½-inch ball of black fondant

tools

Bubble tea straw or wooden
skewer (optional)

Piping bag fitted with a
French open star tip

Wooden skewer cut into
4-inch pieces

Piping bag fitted with a chrysanthemum tip (I use Wilton 81)

Flower nail

2-inch square of parchment paper

1. Prepare the cake. Preheat the oven to 350°F. Prepare the cake batter following the recipe instructions. Split the batter evenly between the three prepared cake pans and bake for 15 to 18 minutes, Check for doneness every 5 minutes, as the layer cakes will bake faster than the sports ball pan cake; cakes are done when a wooden skewer inserted in the middle comes out clean. Let cool completely, then chill the cakes in the refrigerator for 30 minutes.

2. Reserve ¼ cup of the buttercream in a small bowl for the cactus flower. Color the remaining buttercream with the green gel color.

3. Level, fill, and frost your cake to the crumb coat stage (see page 4) using the green buttercream and using the half sports ball cake layer as the top. (Optional: Insert a bubble tea straw or wooden skewer into the center of the three layers to give them some sturdiness for frosting.) Chill the crumb-coated cake in the fridge or freezer for 30 minutes.

4. Fill a piping bag fitted with a French open star tip with the remaining green buttercream.

5. Pipe the cactus. Starting at the bottom of the cake, slowly and steadily pipe a line of green buttercream all the way to the top center of the cake. Continue piping lines of buttercream, nestled closely, until the entire cake has been covered.

6. Make the fondant arms. Clean and dry your hands completely. Divide the white (or green) fondant in two. Between your palms,

roll each piece into a thick log about 3 inches long. Bend each log into an L shape. Insert a wooden skewer piece into each L, making sure there's enough skewer to successfully anchor the arms in place (you will want to insert at least 2 inches into the cake). Gently push the skewered fondant arms into the sides of the cake, with one arm facing up, one arm facing down. Now carefully pipe the fondant arms with lines of green buttercream until they are covered.

7. Tint the reserved buttercream with the red gel color; for such a small amount, you can mix it vigorously with a small spoon. Fill a piping bag fitted with a chrysanthemum tip with the red buttercream.

8. Make the cactus flower. Pipe a tiny amount of the red buttercream onto the flower nail; stick the parchment paper square on top. Pipe a circle of buttercream in the center of the square. Pipe petals around the edge of the circle, pulling upward at the ends, creating little petals that look like scoops. Pipe another round of petals inside and overlapping the first layer, then another layer of petals inside and overlapping the second layer, until you have formed a cactusy-looking flower. Sprinkle the center with white sugar pearls, then place the flower in the freezer for 15 minutes, until set. Gently lift the flower from the parchment paper and place it on the center top of your cactus, covering the point where all the buttercream lines meet.

9. Make the fondant face. With clean and dry hands, using a small amount of cornstarch to prevent stickiness, reserve a tiny amount of the black fondant for the mouth

and form the remaining black fondant into two equal-size balls for the eyes. Flatten the balls and then press them gently into the buttercream just above the halfway mark, setting them 2½ inches apart. (If you feel your eyes might be too heavy for the buttercream to hold them, you can anchor them using wooden skewers cut to size.) Next, make a little black fondant smile by rolling a small amount into a snake shape and placing it midway between and ¼ inch lower than the eyes, pressing it into the buttercream to adhere.

TIPS If you mess up frosting the fondant arms the first time, don't panic! Simply remove the arms, wipe away the buttercream with a clean paper towel, and try again!

You may want to pipe a few practice chrysanthemum flowers, then choose the prettiest one for the cake. Feel free to also use more than one flower to adorn the cactus. Extra flowers can be stored in an airtight container for up to 1 month in the freezer. They are great for adding cute flair to future cakes!

KAWAII PINEAPPLE CAKE

for the cake base

1 recipe cake of your choice
(page 146–48)

Three 8 by 2-inch round cake pans

for the cake decoration

1 recipe (about 4 to 5 cups) Simple
Vanilla Buttercream (page 149)

½ teaspoon gel food color in
lemon yellow

2-inch ball of black fondant

tools

Piping bag fitted with a French
open star tip

My dad's enduring love for Hawaii is very well-known among our family and friends (you'll find him in a Hawaiian shirt more often than not, particularly in the summer months). So for his seventieth birthday, of course we threw him a Hawaiian-themed party, and I made this kawaii smile pineapple cake. This happy chappy works just as well for a first birthday party as it does for a seventieth—or for any tropical-themed celebration.

1. Prepare the cake. Bake the three layers of cake according to the recipe instructions. Tint the buttercream with the yellow gel color.

2. Level, fill, and frost your cake to the crumb coat stage (see page 4) with the tinted buttercream.

3. Fill your piping bag fitted with the French open star tip with the remaining buttercream.

4. Pipe the pineapple. Starting at the bottom edge of the cake, hold the piping bag at a 90-degree angle against the cake and squeeze in short spurts to create a line of frosting dots from bottom to top. Continue piping lines all the way around the cake, nestling the lines closely together, until the sides of the cake are covered. Pipe the top of the cake in the same manner until the entire exterior is covered in frosting.

5. Make the fondant features. Clean and dry your hands completely. Pull a ¼-inch ball off the black fondant. Roll it between your palms to create a small snakelike piece and form it into a U shape to make the smiley face. With the remaining black fondant, make two eyes following the instructions on page 11. Place the black fondant eyes into the sides of the cake; you want the eyes far enough apart to look "cute" but not so far apart that he starts to resemble a fish or an alien. Gently push them into the buttercream to adhere. Place the smile in the same way, gently pushing it into the piped buttercream. Add the pineapple stem to finish the cake (see Crafty Finishes).

CRAFTY FINISHES

Pineapple stem and speech bubble

With **scissors,** use the **template** (page 162) or freehand cut a pineapple stem from a piece of **green craft paper. Tape** the pineapple stem to a **wooden skewer** and insert it into the top center of the piped cake. Try to avoid having the craft paper pineapple stem touch the buttercream—the oil from the buttercream may creep up the paper and stain it. A **speech bubble** (templates, page 161) adds an extra cartoony feel to this pineapple guy and allows you to include a special message.

Pineapple wearing sunglasses

Using the **template** (page 161) and **scissors,** cut out sunglasses from a piece of **purple craft paper.** Cut lenses from a piece of **black felt** and **glue** them to the paper sunglasses. Fold the arms of the sunglasses, then tape **half** of a **wooden skewer** to the inside of each arm. Insert the skewers in the cake so the sunglasses rest on top of the fondant eyes.

STRAWBERRY CAKE

Celebrate a summer birthday with this bright pop of fruity color, or make "strawberries" the theme of the whole party. I bake this cake in a single heightened layer, which makes this project delightfully simple. You can also make this a strawberry-flavored cake by adding ½ cup of strawberry jam to the Vanilla Cream Cake batter, just after you add the eggs. Look for a less-sweet jam or a double fruit variety, or make your own puree by blending 6 large washed and hulled strawberries, 1½ tablespoons of sugar (or to taste), and a pinch of salt until completely pureed. Straw-berry fields forever!

1. Prepare the cake. Make the cake batter and pour into a prepared heart-shaped cake pan, filling it three-quarters full. Bake for 25 minutes, then begin checking for doneness every 2 minutes. Cake is fully baked when a toothpick inserted into the center comes out clean. Remove from the oven and let it cool completely on a wire rack.

2. Tint the buttercream with the pink gel color. Level, fill, and frost your cake to the crumb coat stage (see page 4) with the tinted buttercream.

3. Fill the piping bag fitted with the French open star tip with the remaining pink buttercream.

4. Pipe the strawberry with drop stars. Starting at the bottom edge of the cake, hold the piping bag at a 90-degree angle against the cake and squeeze and release the piping bag in short spurts to create a line of frosting stars from bottom to top. Continue piping lines all the way around the cake, nestling the lines closely together, until the sides of the cake are covered. Pipe the top of the cake in the same manner until the entire exterior is covered in buttercream drop stars.

5. Press the white chocolate chips into the cake to emulate strawberry seeds, leaving an inch or so between each. Finish by adding a strawberry stem (see Crafty Finishes).

TIP If you want a red strawberry cake instead of a pink one, you will need a fair amount of red gel color to achieve the proper shade. Start with 4 teaspoons of red gel food color and add more as needed. Note that buttercream tinted with gel color gets brighter and more color concentrated over time, so add additional color slowly.

CRAFTY FINISHES

Strawberry stem

Using the **template** (page 160) and a pair of scissors, cut a strawberry stem from a piece of **green craft paper. Tape** the stem to a **wooden skewer.** Gently insert it into the top of the heart cake. The paper may soak up the buttercream if they're touching; to avoid this, place the stem in just before presenting and serving.

BURGER CAKE

for the cake base

1 recipe Vanilla Cream Cake (page 146)

½ recipe One Bowl Dark Chocolate Cake (page 147)

Three 8 by 2-inch round cake pans

for the cake decoration

1 recipe (about 4 to 5 cups) Simple Vanilla Buttercream (page 149)

¼ teaspoon gel food color in green

¼ teaspoon gel food color in yellow

1 teaspoon (or more) gel food color in red

¼ cup Vanilla Simple Syrup (see page 85)

White sugar pearls (see Resources, page 164) or white fondant punched out into small circles, using a piping tip as a cutter

tools

Piping bag fitted with an open star tip

Piping bag fitted with a leaf tip

Piping bag fitted with a medium-size open circle tip

Piping bag fitted with a large open circle tip

Pastry brush

Cake board

Cake turntable

I first made this burger cake several years ago for my own trompe l'oeil–themed birthday party. All the guests (and the birthday girl, too!) made trick-of-the-eye food—that is, food that looks like one thing but is actually something entirely different. I got to judge the items based on creativity, taste, and presentation. Some of the dishes at the party included churro cinnamon sugar "fries" with strawberry jam "ketchup" (nice one, Rich!) and my personal favorite and the winner, "hot dogs" made of split Twinkies, log candy, and shredded coconut dyed green to mimic relish. Of course, the baker/birthday girl had to deliver too—so this burger cake it was. The soda cup and French fries paper cake toppers are optional, of course, but I think they give the cake an extra cute boost. I've also made a version of this cake with thin squares of orange fondant for "cheese" and a green fondant "pickle" on top—customize this burger to your heart's content!

Note: For an extra-cute presentation, cover your own cake board (see page 5) with a retro-feel red-and-white-striped craft paper.

1. Prepare the cake. Preheat the oven to 350°F. Make the cake batters according to the recipe instructions. Divide the vanilla cream cake batter evenly between two of the prepared cake pans. Pour the half recipe of chocolate cake batter into the third prepared cake pan. Use an offset spatula to level the batter. Bake for 20 minutes, check for doneness, and continue baking until a toothpick inserted into the center of each layer comes out clean and the cakes are springy to the touch. Let them cool completely on wire racks.

2. Divide the buttercream in half. Set aside one bowl. Divide the contents of the second bowl evenly among three smaller bowls. Mix the green gel color into the first bowl, yellow into the second bowl, and red into the third bowl. Note: sometimes "red" is a difficult color to achieve with buttercream, so add the gel in small increments until you get your desired shade.

3. Fill a piping bag fitted with an open star tip with the uncolored buttercream. Fill a piping bag fitted with a leaf tip with the green buttercream. Fill a piping bag fitted with a

medium-size round tip with the yellow buttercream. Finally, fill a piping bag fitted with a large round tip with the red buttercream.

4. Place a covered cake board on a cake turntable. Pipe a dab of uncolored buttercream onto the cake board. Level the first vanilla cake layer (see page 5), then place it cut side up in the center of the cake board. Starting from the outside and working your way in toward the middle, pipe the uncolored buttercream in concentric circles, creating a giant, generous swirl of buttercream. Stop when you get to the center.

5. Level the chocolate cake layer, then place it cut side down on top of the vanilla buttercream. Pipe the next layer of uncolored buttercream just as you did the first layer.

6. Next, begin piping green buttercream "lettuce" right on top of the uncolored buttercream layer, using the piping bag with the leaf tip. The idea is not to be too uniform with your leaves! Squeeze the piping bag a little harder to get bigger leaves, and overlap and layer them in a way that looks organic.

7. Squiggle on your "mustard" using the yellow buttercream. I pipe large loops all along the exterior, on top of the lettuce layer but not covering it.

8. Use the red buttercream for your ketchup, piping this in an ongoing loop on top of the yellow buttercream layer but in between the yellow loops.

9. Carefully place the final vanilla cake layer, unleveled and dome side up, on top of the "ketchup" buttercream. Gently press down to adhere.

10. Using a pastry brush, brush the top of the cake dome with vanilla simple syrup. While the syrup is still sticky, place the white sugar pearls or white fondant circles all over the top of the dome to emulate a sesame seed bun.

TIPS Swiss meringue buttercream doesn't hold its color as well as the simple vanilla buttercream, so I'd use the simple recipe for this cake. If you will be serving this on a hot day, frost the cake in an air-conditioned environment and keep the cake in the fridge until 30 minutes before presentation.

VANILLA SIMPLE SYRUP

1 cup water

1 cup granulated sugar

1 teaspoon vanilla extract

In a small saucepan, bring the water and the sugar to boil over high heat, stirring the sugar until it dissolves. Once the water boils, remove the mixture from the heat and let it sit until it is cool and has thickened slightly. I speed this up by refrigerating it for an hour. Then, add the vanilla extract and stir to combine. It will keep in the fridge for up to 1 month.

Simple syrup can also be great for remoistening a cake that's been slightly overbaked: just remove the cake from the pan, let it cool, and use a pastry brush to brush on some simple syrup.

CRAFTY FINISHES

Soda and Fries Toppers

Using the **templates** (page 163) and a pair of **scissors,** cut out the French fry shapes from **yellow craft paper,** the carton from **red-and-white-striped craft paper,** the soda cup from **green and white craft paper,** and the straw from striped craft paper. Glue the pieces together using a **glue stick. Tape** the fries and the soda to separate **wooden skewers** and insert them into the cake.

PRETTY CAKES

RAINBOW INSIDE AND OUT CAKE

for the cake base

1 recipe Vanilla Cream Cake
(page 146)

Five 7 by 2-inch round cake pans

for the cake decoration

1 recipe (about 6 cups) Vanilla Swiss
Meringue Buttercream (page 151)

¼ teaspoon each gel food color
in purple, blue, green,
yellow, and pink

tools

5 disposable piping bags
(no piping tips)

Cake turntable

Cake bench scraper

I made this cake with a big idea in mind: that goodness can prevail in the world. This cake represents positive light and energy, goodness worldwide, acceptance of all people, hope, and change. It works marvelously for any special celebration, whether it's a tenth birthday party, a coming-out party, or a wedding. It is magic on the inside and out.

1. Prepare the cake. Preheat the oven to 350°F. Make the cake batter according to the recipe instructions. Divide the batter evenly between 5 medium-size bowls. Color each bowl of batter with one of the gel colors and pour each colored batter into its own pre-pared cake pan. Use an offset spatula to level the batter. Bake for 15 minutes and check for doneness. Continue baking and checking every 2 minutes until a toothpick inserted into the center of each cake layer comes out clean. Let the layers cool completely on wire racks.

2. Following the rainbow's ROYGBIV concept, level, fill, and frost the cake to the crumb coat stage (see page 4) using un-colored buttercream. I like to start with the purple layer on the bottom, then blue, green, yellow, and pink as the top layer. Chill in the fridge or freezer until the frosting is set, about 30 minutes.

3. Divide the remaining buttercream evenly into five medium-size bowls. Tint each bowl of buttercream with its own gel color, folding the gel color in with a spatula or spoon. Swiss meringue buttercream doesn't absorb gel color as well as simple buttercream, so you may need a little more than you think to achieve vibrant colors. Or you can keep the color scheme pastel—still very cute!

4. Fill each piping bag with a different color of buttercream. With scissors, snip the end off each bag, about ½ inch from the tip.

5. Pipe the cake. Place the cake on the cake turntable. Starting from the bottom of the cake, pipe the buttercream around the sides in even horizontal rows, slowly turning the cake as you pipe. Begin with the purple buttercream for the first row and work your way up the cake with blue, green, yellow, and finally pink, in the order of the rainbow—the same sequence as your stacked cake layers.

6. Now, take your cake bench scraper and position it at a perpendicular angle against the cake. Begin smoothing the buttercream, turning the cake as you go and scraping the excess frosting into an empty bowl. Make as

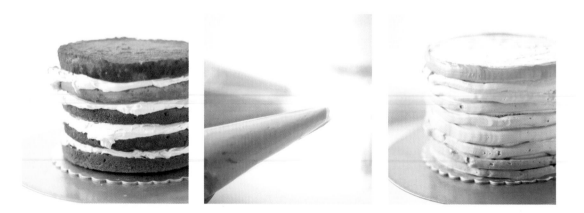

Rainbow topper

To make the rainbow topper, use a **3-inch circle punch** to punch a circle from a piece of **pink craft paper**. Cut the circle in half using **scissors**. From **yellow, green, blue, and purple craft paper,** hand cut semicircles in descending sizes. **Glue** the pieces onto the pink half circle to form a rainbow, leaving the pink as the top edge. Then, with sharp scissors, cut out a little half circle from the bottom purple row to form the U-shaped base of the rainbow. **Tape** the rainbow to a **wooden skewer** and insert it into the center of the cake.

many turns of the cake as you need in order to create the smooth rainbow stripes. If you find there's a hole, add a tiny amount of the missing color and smooth it again to fill.

7. Finally, pipe the top of the cake with buttercream "kisses" (or, as I call them, blobettes). Use the rest of the buttercream in varying colors to cover the top of the cake, alternating colors as you see fit.

RAINBOW ROSETTE CAKE

for the cake base

1 recipe Vanilla Cream Cake
(page 146)

¼ teaspoon each gel food color
in electric pink, lemon yellow,
sky blue, and violet

Four 7 by 2-inch round cake pans

for the cake decoration

1½ recipes (about 7 to 8 cups)
Simple Vanilla Buttercream (page
149) or 1¼ recipes (about 8 cups)
Vanilla Swiss Meringue Buttercream (page 151)

¼ teaspoon each gel food color
in electric pink, sky blue, and
lemon yellow

tools

Piping bag fitted with an
open star tip

Making this show-stopping Rainbow Rosette Cake is much easier than meets the eye. The buttercream rosettes are made up of three pastel colors sneakily combined into one piping bag fitted with a single open star piping tip. When any of the complementary colors mix, they form even more colors, creating the loveliest hues. I like taking this cake over the top by baking my cake layers in multiple colors for an extra surprise inside.

1. Prepare the cake. Preheat the oven to 350°F. Make the cake batter according to the recipe instructions. Divide the batter evenly between 4 medium-size bowls. Color each bowl of batter with one of the gel colors; pour each colored batter into its own prepared cake pan. Use an offset spatula to level the batter. Bake for 16 to 18 minutes and check for doneness. Continue baking and checking every 2 minutes until a toothpick inserted into the center of the cakes comes out clean. Let cool completely on wire racks.

2. Level, fill, and frost your cake to the crumb coat stage (see page 4) using the uncolored buttercream.

3. Divide the remaining buttercream equally among three medium-size bowls. Tint each bowl of buttercream with an individual color—pink, blue, or yellow.

4. Fill a piping bag fitted with an open star tip with the three colored buttercreams, carefully spooning each color side by side into the bag so all three colors will flow out at the same time (see page 8). Gently squeeze the piping bag so the colors reach the tip and pipe out a burst of buttercream on a side plate or piece of parchment paper to get things flowing.

5. Pipe the rosettes. Starting at the bottom of the cake, hold the piping bag at a 45-degree angle to the cake. Squeeze the bag while moving it in a counterclockwise circular motion, forming a rosette. Stop squeezing and pull the bag away, creating a little "tail" on the rosette. Continue piping rosettes along the bottom row, beginning each new rosette on top of the tail of the last one. Pipe rosettes in this fashion all the way around the cake.

6. Begin piping a second row by slightly offsetting the first new rosette in between two rosettes on the bottom row. Continue piping rosettes around the cake, creating rows all the way to the top edge.

7. On the top of the cake, begin piping rosettes in circles, starting from the outside edge and working your way inward. Continue piping until you reach the center.

TIP Reposition the piping bag in your hands as you pipe the rosettes. I like to pipe a rosette, then slightly turn the bag in my hands for the next rosette. This will give you an overall rainbow effect rather than creating rosettes that look exactly the same.

CRAFTY FINISHES

Hello there, cake!

I like to finish this cake with a typographical element to break up the floweriness of the rosettes. Use a **circle paper punch** of your choice to punch out a circle from a piece of **pink craft paper**. Stamp the circle with a **"Hello" stamp** (or your choice of typography stamp) and **tape** the circle to a **wooden skewer**. Insert it into the cake alongside a **washi tape flag** (page 116) in a complementary color.

MERINGUE PARTY CAKE

for the cake base

**1 recipe cake of your choice
(pages 146–48)**

Three 8 by 2-inch round cake pans

for the cake decoration

**1 recipe (about 4 to 5 cups) Simple
Vanilla Buttercream (page 149)**

⅛ teaspoon gel food color in teal

**⅛ teaspoon gel food color in
sky blue**

**1 recipe Swiss Meringue Kisses
(page 157), tinted in
a variety of colors**

tools

**Piping bag fitted with a
French open star tip**

I love the charming presence of crisp, cutely shaped meringues on top of a buttercream-frosted cake. They add color, modernity, and texture. You can also crush them up into chewy, crunchy crumbs and use them like sprinkles. I detail how to make Swiss Meringue Kisses on page 157, which includes a simple recipe. Your piping tip will determine the meringue shape, piped out just as you would a buttercream drop star.

1. Prepare the cake. Bake the three layers of cake according to the recipe instructions.

2. Reserve ½ cup of the uncolored vanilla buttercream for piping the borders. Tint the remaining buttercream using the teal and sky blue gel colors, blending each color in gradually until you achieve the desired shade.

3. Level, fill, and frost your cake with to the final coat stage (see page 6) with the tinted turquoise buttercream.

4. Fill the piping bag fitted with a French open star tip with the uncolored buttercream. Create a shell border along the top and bottom edges of the cake by holding the piping bag at a 45-degree angle against the cake, squeezing the bag, and then pulling away, leaving a little tail. Pipe the next shell on top of the tail, and continue along in this fashion until the entire top and bottom edges have been piped.

5. Using your colorful mix of meringue kisses, gently press the meringues on top of the cake in a somewhat uniform manner, nestling them pretty close together and alternating the colors accordingly to your liking.

6. Place a few meringue kisses in a small plastic zip-top bag or between two pieces of plastic wrap. Gently crush them with either your hands or a rolling pin. "Sprinkle" the bottom shell border with the crushed meringue bits to add color and texture.

TIP Meringues will lose their crispiness over time when they are exposed to moisture. If possible, place the meringues on your cake no more than an hour before serving for the most crispy results! Alternatively, don't cry over slightly softened meringues—they still serve as an adorably artful cake topper, adding color and form. Serve leftover meringues in a pretty dish or place them in candy bags to use as party favors.

CRAFTY FINISHES

Circle flag

This cake calls for some **washi tape flags** (page 116) in varying heights and a cute circle birthday message, which I made with my **2-inch circle craft punch, craft paper,** and one of my **alphabet stamp sets.**

MODERN CANDY PARTY CAKE

I made this cake for my sweet pals in the band Black Mountain. They were performing a hometown show after many months of touring on the road. Lots of friends were going to be there, and it just felt like a celebration. A spectacular cake was in order: mauve-tinted buttercream, dark chocolate cake layers, a perfect painterly drip of shiny ganache, and bright pops of color on top. It takes a little restraint not to cover the entire cake with candies, buttercream, and sprinkles, but either way, it's a lot of fun to make and even more fun to share with your favorite folks.

1. Prepare the cake. Bake the three layers of cake according to the recipe instructions.

2. Divide the buttercream into three bowls as follows: place ¼ cup in each of two bowls and the remaining buttercream in the third. Tint the larger portion of buttercream using the electric purple gel color (or a mixture of purple and pink).

3. Level, fill, and frost your cake to the final coat stage (see page 6) with the purple buttercream. Chill the cake in the fridge or freezer for 20 minutes.

4. Make the chocolate ganache. Prepare the chocolate ganache according to the recipe directions. Let the ganache cool slightly; it will thicken as it cools. You want it to be thin enough to drip but not so thin that the drips won't stick. I power chill the ganache in the freezer until it's still dripable but cool to the touch. Test it every 5 to 10 minutes by spooning it up and watching it drip back down; it's ready when it coats the back of a spoon easily and drips slowly.

5. Using a small spoon and a very small amount of ganache to start with—about ¼ teaspoon—drip the ganache from the top edge of the chilled cake down the side. If your drip cascades down too fast and hits the bottom (and you don't like this look), chill your ganache for a few minutes longer. If your drip is too short, add a little more ganache to the same drip, a tiny amount at a time. While you are making the drips, also create a dam of ganache around the top of the cake: spoon ganache around the cake's perimeter so it meets up with the drips but

doesn't drip down itself. Continue spooning the ganache in this manner all the way around the cake.

6. Now, carefully pour a small amount of ganache at a time on the top of the cake and spread it with an offset spatula until it meets the ganache dam. Add more as needed to cover the top of the cake entirely. Power chill the cake in the freezer for 15 minutes to set the ganache.

7. Tint the remaining small bowls of buttercream using the electric pink and teal colors; start with ⅛ teaspoon of gel color for each and add more until you achieve the shades you desire. Fit each piping bag with an open star tip. Fill the first piping bag with the pink buttercream and the second piping bag with the teal buttercream.

8. Alternate piping drop stars and rosettes in varying colors across the top of the cake. Add the raspberries and fancy candies wherever you see fit. If you find one side of your cake is looking visually heavier than the other, balance it by adding candies, rosettes, or raspberries to the opposite side. Finish the cake with a light dusting of sprinkles!

MINI MODERN PARTY CAKES

I love the look of these Mini Modern Party Cakes—they're a cute update on the traditional cupcake. The principle is still the same: small, dainty, and, most important, covered in frosting and sprinkles!

for the cake base

1 recipe Vanilla Cream Cake (page 146)

2 miniloaf baking pans (I use an 8-cavity miniloaf pan)

Vegetable oil cooking spray

for the cake decoration

1 recipe (about 4 to 5 cups) Simple Vanilla Buttercream (page 149)

¼ teaspoon gel food color in electric pink

¼ teaspoon gel food color in teal

Organic unsprayed edible flowers

Candied flowers (see page 135)

Candies of your choice

Sprinkles

tools

Piping bag fitted with an open star tip

Piping bag fitted with a French open star tip

1. Prepare the cake. Preheat the oven to 350°F. Make the cake batter according to the recipe instructions. Prepare the miniloaf pans by lightly spritzing them with vegetable oil cooking spray to prevent sticking. Using a retractable ice cream scoop for ease, fill each cavity two-thirds full with cake batter; baking time will depend on cavity size. Bake on the middle rack for 10 to 14 minutes, until a toothpick inserted in the middle of each loaf comes out clean, turning the pans once halfway through to ensure even baking. Let the miniloaves cool in their pans for 5 minutes, then turn out onto wire racks to cool completely.

2. Using a serrated bread knife, level any "dome" that has baked up above the sides of the loaf pans. Place loaves cut side down on a plate to decorate them.

3. Split the buttercream evenly between two medium-size bowls. Tint half of the buttercream pink and the other half, teal. Fill the piping bag fitted with an open star tip with the pink buttercream. Fill the piping bag fitted with the French open star tip with the teal buttercream.

4. Let your creativity flow! Pipe drop stars, lines, and rosettes in alternating colors of buttercream. Add edible flowers or petals, candied flowers, candies, and sprinkles to each loaf.

TIP Serve your Mini Modern Party Cakes on vintage tea party plates or line them up on a serving platter and decorate the platter with more flowers.

BUTTERCREAM FLOWER POWER CAKE

for the cake base

**1 recipe cake of your choice
(pages 146–48)**

Three 8 by 2-inch round cake pans

for the cake decoration

**1½ recipes (about 7 to 8 cups)
Simple Vanilla Buttercream
(page 149)**

**½ teaspoon gel food color in
electric pink**

⅛ teaspoon gel food color in teal

⅛ teaspoon gel food color in violet

**⅛ teaspoon gel food color in
leaf green**

tools

Piping bag fitted with a petal tip

**2 piping bags fitted with
open star tips**

**Piping bag fitted with a French
open star tip**

Piping bag fitted with a leaf tip

Flower nail

2-inch parchment paper squares

The local bakery's buttercream-rose diplomat cake has been coveted in our family for generations; a rose-topped slice of this puff pastry and liquor-soaked butter cake always signifies a special occasion. So when I started baking cakes more than a decade ago, my first obsession was with buttercream roses. Steeped in nostalgia, they looked so complex to me. There are many different methods out there for making them, but I like the single-piping-tip technique: using a petal tip (Wilton 104), I pipe a tight scroll of buttercream as the center, then I pipe the outlying layers of petals from there. It makes a modern and cute rose, but with a vintage vibe. The sneaky little secret to working with buttercream flowers is to freeze them until they're solid, making them easy as pie to handle.

I love the wild jumble of piped flowers and leaves on this cake—a modern update of my beloved buttercream roses, with the minimalist sides contrasting nicely against the maximum flower blast on top. But you could also go all out and cover the entire cake with flowers!

1. Prepare the cake. Bake the three layers of cake according to the recipe instructions. Level, fill, and frost your cake to the final coat stage (see page 000) with the uncolored vanilla buttercream. Set the cake aside.

2. In a small bowl, mix 2 cups of buttercream with the electric pink gel color. Divide the remaining buttercream into three small bowls, adding teal gel color to one, violet to the second, and leaf green to the third.

3. Fill the piping bag fitted with a petal tip with some of the pink buttercream, reserving the rest. Pipe a tiny dab of buttercream onto the flower nail; place the parchment paper square on top, pressing lightly to adhere.

4. Pipe the buttercream roses. First, pipe a tight center scroll for the rose. The petal tip has a teardrop shape. Holding the piping bag at a 45-degree angle to the flower nail with the wide end of the teardrop on the bottom, squeeze the piping bag and turn the flower nail at the same time to form the center of the rose.

5. Next, pipe the first layer of petals. Squeeze the piping bag while at the same time turning the flower nail and make a slight down-up-down "rainbow" shape for the petal. Pipe the next petal in the same way, overlapping slightly, and then pipe a third, so there are three total around the center scroll. Continue piping layers of petals until you have reached the desired size for your rose (mine have three layers of petals). For larger roses, pipe an additional layer. Carefully remove the parchment paper from the flower

nail with the rose attached and place it on a baking sheet or flat plate. Repeat the process until you've made as many roses as you want (I made about a dozen for this cake). Once done, freeze the plate, uncovered, for at least 20 minutes, until the roses are cold and firm to the touch. To store any extras, freeze until firm, then transfer to an airtight container. They will keep in the freezer for up to 1 month.

6. Fill one of the piping bags fitted with an open star tip with the reserved pink buttercream and the other with the teal buttercream. Fill your piping bag fitted with a French open star tip with the violet buttercream. Finally, fill the piping bag fitted with a leaf tip with the green buttercream.

7. Time to assemble your floral cake! I like to go for a balance of color and flowers, and I tend to work without a completely final look in mind. Remove your roses from the freezer and gently press them into the top of the cake to adhere, spacing them apart so they're not all concentrated in one area. Using the pink, teal, and violet buttercreams, pipe drop stars and rosettes here and there to break up the large roses; don't forget to add little piped leaves with the green buttercream! I like to nestle the flowers quite closely together for a nice grouping of colors and piped textures. You can also place roses one at a time and pipe around each as you go; just make sure to keep the roses cold and firm for your own ease. Any "naked" spots can be piped in with green leaves.

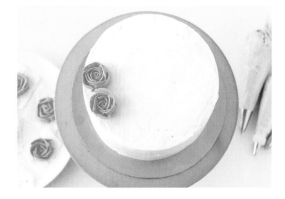

TIP Don't panic if you place your rose down on the cake and you're not happy with where it's sitting. Use an offset spatula and your fingers to gently lift the rose off. Refreeze it if necessary or discard if it got bungled up somehow. If you left a thick smear of buttercream behind, use an offset spatula to flatten and smooth it down, then simply pipe a rosette on top. It's easy to cover any mucked-up buttercream!

variation

FRUIT AND FLOWERS CRESCENT CAKE

This vibrant, modern cake beauty was inspired by the floral crescent cakes created by Nikki Lee of Unbirthday Bakery in Sydney, Australia. I love the artful manner in which she combines bright colors with piping, chocolate gems, and fresh petals. Here I went for deep, dark chocolate layers against a turquoise blue buttercream for high impact, but this cake would also be pretty showstopping with hot pink vanilla cake layers!

1. Prepare the cake. Bake the three layers of cake according to the recipe instructions.

2. Place ½ cup of vanilla buttercream in a small bowl and tint it pink with the electric pink gel color. Tint the remaining buttercream with a mixture of the teal and sky blue gel colors.

3. Level, fill, and frost your cake to the final coat stage (see page 6) using the blue buttercream.

4. Fill the piping bag fitted with a French open star tip with the pink buttercream. Fill the piping bag fitted with an open star tip with the blue buttercream.

5. Use your piping bags with the pink and blue buttercreams to begin piping a unique cake border—a mixture of shells and drop stars on top of the cake (see page 7). To create the crescent look, fill a crescent-moon-shaped area of the cake with decor, leaving the rest blank. Pipe drop stars and minirosettes (see page 8) into the crescent shape using the pink buttercream and pipe drop stars using the blue buttercream, alternating with fresh raspberries. Place torn pink carnation petals in an even yet haphazard design, then lightly dust the cake with sprinkles. Place a raspberry in the center. Reserve additional raspberries for placing on top of each slice of cake for a look inspired by the cake painter Wayne Thiebaud.

6. Using the remaining blue buttercream, pipe a ruffly border around the bottom of the cake.

CRAFTY FINISHES

Washi tape flags

Finish the cake with washi tape flags and letter-stamped circle flags (see page 100) in matching or complementary colors—always a welcome modern contrast to the floral vibe of the cake! Cutting a 2-inch piece of **washi tape**, fold it in half over a **wooden skewer** so that it sticks to itself. Use sharp **scissors** to make a V-shaped cut in the tape, giving it a flag look.

TYPOGRAPHY LOVE CAKE

for the cake base

1 recipe cake of your choice
(pages 146–48)

Three 8 by 2-inch round cake pans

for the cake decoration

1 recipe (about 4 to 5 cups) Simple
Vanilla Buttercream (page 149)

⅛ teaspoon gel food color in violet

½ teaspoon gel food color in teal

Rainbow sprinkles

1 package (8 oz) candy melts
(see Resources, page 164) or
white chocolate

tools

Piping bag fitted with an open star
tip (I use a French multipronged
open star tip)

Silicone alphabet letter molds
(see Resources, page 164)

Wooden skewer

I met my husband over sixteen years ago now. A close friend from my university days decided to set me up on a blind date with one of her pals, a tall white guy in a black jean jacket and red Converse sneakers who played in a heavy metal band. He was also finishing his honors thesis in the social construction of binary gender—plus he was cute! Ten-plus years of marriage and plenty of storms later, we are still hanging in there, now a little family. This cake is an homage to love in all of its magic and complexities. It's a simple but high-impact cake with chocolate letters made using a silicone alphabet letter mold.

1. Prepare the cake. Bake the three layers of cake according to the recipe instructions.

2. Place ½ cup of the buttercream into a small bowl and tint it with the violet gel color. Tint the remaining buttercream with the teal gel color. Level, fill, and frost your cake to the final coat stage (see page 6) with the teal buttercream.

3. Fill the piping bag fitted with an open star tip with the violet buttercream. Pipe a shell border around the bottom of the cake: holding the piping bag at a 90-degree angle against the cake, squeeze the bag and pull away, leaving a bulbous shell shape and a little buttercream tail. Pipe the next shell on top of the tail, and continue piping around the cake in this manner until the ends of the shell

border meet up. Create a shell border around the top edge of the cake in the same way. Decorate the borders by dusting lightly with sprinkles.

4. Melt the candy melts according to the package instructions. When the candy melts are liquid, carefully spoon into the alphabet letter molds in the letters of your choice (I used L-O-V-E, but you can use whatever you like). With a wooden skewer, pop any air bubbles in your letters and ensure there are no air pockets. Chill the molds in the freezer for 15 to 20 minutes, until the letters are completely hardened.

5. Pop the letters out of the molds. Handle them gingerly, as the heat from your hands may make them a little melty looking. Gently press your L-O-V-E letters into the top of the buttercream-frosted cake.

TIPS If you are using white chocolate to make your letters, melt it gently over a double boiler on low heat. I don't recommend coloring white chocolate yourself, as chocolate can seize when mishandled. For cute colored letters, use colored prepackaged candy melts—they make it easy!

CRAFTY FINISHES

Paper hearts

Using a **heart-shaped paper punch** or **scissors**, punch or cut out small hearts from **pink craft paper**. Tape the hearts to **wooden skewers** and insert them in the cake.

POM-POM PARTY CAKE

for the cake base

1 recipe Vanilla Cream Cake
(page 146)

Three 8 by 2-inch round cake pans

¼ teaspoon gel food color in pink

¼ teaspoon gel food color in yellow

¼ teaspoon gel food color in
sky blue

for the cake decoration

1 recipe (about 4 to 5 cups) Simple
Vanilla Buttercream (page 149)

¼ teaspoon gel food color in pink

¼ teaspoon gel food color in yellow

¼ teaspoon gel food color
in sky blue

tools

3 piping bags, each fitted with a
multi-opening tip, or use a mix of
piping tips (such as 1 multi-
opening tip, 1 open star tip, and
1 French open star tip)

You could say I am obsessed with the multi-opening tip—I use it to make fur, grass, and artful hairiness. I think it just looks so hilariously vintage, and I love the texture it creates. It also makes the cutest buttercream pom-poms that a cake ever did see. This cake wavers between a pointillist modern art look and a "Cousin It" theme, as though it might very well slink off its cake stand and scuttle off somewhere. Everyone loves a surprise inside, too—matching cake layers? Why not!

1. Prepare the cake. Preheat the oven to 350°F. Make the cake batter according to the recipe instructions. Divide the batter evenly between 3 medium-size bowls. Tint each bowl of batter with one of the gel colors. Pour each colored batter into its own prepared cake pan, using an offset spatula to level the batter. Bake according to the recipe instructions. Let the layers cool completely on wire racks.

2. Level, fill, and frost your multicolored layer cake to the crumb coat stage (see page 4) using the vanilla buttercream.

3. Divide the remaining buttercream equally among 3 medium bowls. Add the pink gel color to the first bowl, the yellow gel color to the second bowl, and the sky blue gel color to the third bowl. Mix each color into the buttercream until incorporated.

4. Fill each piping bag fitted with a multi-opening tip with a separate color of buttercream.

5. Pom-pom time! Holding one of the piping bags at a 90-degree angle against the cake, squeeze out and pull away in a short burst for a puffy little pom-pom look. Use one color and pipe a bunch of pom-poms randomly around the cake. Do the same with the second and third colors. Then step back, see which areas need more pink or blue or yellow, and fill them in. Continue in this haphazard way until the entire cake is covered in pom-poms.

TIP If you're personally feeling skeptical about the "pipe where the wind takes you" method, take a deep breath, let go of any inhibitions, pretend you're a kid, and pipe away. In fact, this cake is a lot of fun for kids to work on. Since there's no set design, they can pipe according to their own whimsy.

CRAFTY FINISHES

Circle cake toppers

Using a **small circle punch**, punch out circles in **pink, yellow, and sky blue craft paper** to match the frosting. **Tape** the circles to **cocktail sticks**. Insert them into the cake, evenly spaced and at varying heights.

SURPRISE CHECKER-BOARD CAKE

for the cake base

1 recipe Vanilla Cream Cake (page 146)

½ teaspoon gel food color in electric pink

½ teaspoon gel food color in teal

Four 6 by 2-inch round cake pans

for the cake decoration

1 recipe (about 4 to 5 cups) Simple Vanilla Buttercream (page 149)

Rainbow sprinkles

tools

4-inch cake ring or circle cutter

2-inch cake ring or circle cutter

Two 18 by 13-inch baking sheets lined with parchment paper

Piping bag fitted with a large French multipronged open star tip

Oh, just another unassuming, pristinely frosted white cake with a light dash of sprinkles, right? Wrong! Slice into this cake and you get the cutest little checkerboard pattern in pink and blue, a surprising color blast against the starkness of the exterior. I truly love how sneaky this cake is. Best of all, getting the checkerboard effect is delightfully easy. You could holiday this cake up, too, by making it with red and green squares, or make an eighties-themed cake with black and white squares, a fuchsia pink exterior, and melted chocolate "paint" splatters.

1. Prepare the cake. Preheat the oven to 350°F. Make the cake batter according to the recipe instructions. Divide the batter into two large bowls; tint the batter in one bowl with the electric pink gel color and the batter in the other bowl with the teal gel color. Pour the pink batter into two of the prepared 6-inch cake pans; pour the teal batter into the other two prepared 6-inch cake pans. Bake for 18 to 20 minutes, checking for doneness at 18 minutes using a toothpick inserted into the center of each layer. When the toothpick comes out clean, it's ready. Cool the cakes completely on wire racks (or power chill them in the freezer to cool them more quickly). Once cooled, chill them further by placing the cakes in the freezer for 15 minutes. You want to chill them just long enough to make them easier to cut but not freeze them—making them impossible to cut!

2. Remove the cakes from their pans. Using a serrated bread knife, level the cakes (see page 5).

3. Lay the cakes flat on your work surface. Center the large cake ring or circle cutter on top of the first cake layer and punch out a 4-inch circle. Then, center the small cake ring or circle cutter within this 4-inch circle and punch out a 2-inch round. Repeat this process with each cake layer. You will end up with four 6-inch and four 4-inch pieces that look like car tires plus four 2-inch center circles.

4. Checks, please! Using the parchment paper–lined baking sheets as your work surface, start with one of the 6-inch pink cake

"tires" and spread a thin layer of buttercream along the inside edge. Now, fit a 4-inch blue cake "tire" into the 6-inch pink "tire." Spread a thin layer of frosting along the inside of the blue round and nestle a 2-inch pink cake circle in the center. Continue this method with the other cutout pieces until you've assembled four cake layers, each with alternating color rings. They'll look like cool cake bull's-eyes!

5. Freeze the cake layers for 15 minutes. This will make it easier to handle the layers in the next step.

6. Remove the layers from the freezer and begin assembling and frosting the cake, starting with one of the outermost-pink layers on the bottom, then stacking an outermost-blue layer on top of that, and continuing to alternate the cake layer colors to achieve the checkerboard effect. Handling the layers carefully, fill and frost to the crumb coat stage (see page 4). Chill the cake for 15 minutes in the freezer, then frost again to the final coat stage (see page 6).

7. Fill the piping bag fitted with a large French multipronged open star tip with about ½ cup of the remaining buttercream. Pipe a shell border along the top edge of the cake by squeezing the piping bag and letting a "shell" shape build up, then pulling up and leaving a little "tail" of buttercream. Pipe the next shell on top of the tail and continue piping shells in this manner until you have created a border all the way around the cake. Adorn heartily with rainbow sprinkles.

CRAFTY FINISHES

Letter stickers

I love me some typographical elements, and especially the clean lines of these particular **letter stickers** I found at a local office supplies superstore (they can also be found online; see Resources, page 164). This is the easiest cake topper ever: I simply unpeel the stickers and adhere them to **wooden skewers**, adding **clear tape** to the backs to secure them. Short words work best with a large font such as the one I used on this cake. Look for smaller stickers for a wordier cake message!

CIRCLE GARLAND PARTY CAKE

for the cake base

1 recipe cake of your choice
(pages 146–48)

Three 8 by 2-inch round cake pans

for the cake decoration

1 recipe (about 4 to 5 cups) Simple
Vanilla Buttercream (page 149) or
1 recipe (about 6 cups) Vanilla
Swiss Meringue Buttercream
(page 151)

⅛ teaspoon gel food color in pink

Rainbow sprinkles

tools

Piping bag fitted with an
open star tip

Pretty in pink, and so simple with a dusting of sprinkles, this cake is made modern with a very easy cake garland. It can be made in any shade and would work for a birthday, or baby shower, or even as a collection of wedding cakes on a dessert table. The cake garland is also a simple and cute way to match a party's color scheme!

1. Prepare the cake. Bake the three layers of cake according to the recipe instructions.

2. Tint your buttercream using the pink gel coloring. Level, fill, and frost your cake to the final coat stage (see page 6) with the pink buttercream.

3. Fill the piping bag fitted with an open star tip with the pink buttercream. Pipe a ruffle border along the top edge of the cake this way: Hold the piping bag with your dominant hand at a 45-degree angle to the cake's top edge. Squeeze the bag with medium pressure so that a ridged ball of buttercream forms, then pull gently away, creating a tail. Pipe the next ruffle on top of the tail and continue piping in this manner until the border covers the entire edge. Dust the top of the cake with rainbow sprinkles. Adorn with the Circle Garland (see Crafty Finishes).

Circle garland

Using an array of **craft punches**, punch out some colorful pieces of **craft paper.** Attach each punched-out circle (or shape of your choice) to a string of baker's twine using **washi tape** or **regular tape,** making sure to apply the tape at the top of each circle. Space the paper circles evenly along the twine, then tie each end of the twine to a tall **wooden skewer.** Place the skewers into your cake—now it's time to party!

CANDIED FLOWER CROWN CAKE

for the cake base

1 recipe cake of your choice
(pages 146–48)

Three 8 by 2-inch round cake pans

for the cake decoration

Organic unsprayed edible pansy
flowers and loose petals

2 teaspoons meringue powder
(see Resources, page 164;
I use Wilton brand)

2 tablespoons water

¼ cup superfine sugar (or regular
granulated sugar ground in a
food processor until very fine)

1 recipe (about 4 to 5 cups) Simple
Vanilla Buttercream (page 149)
or 1 recipe (about 6 cups) Vanilla
Swiss Meringue Buttercream
(page 151)

⅛ teaspoon gel food color in pink

Gently washed fresh berries, such
as raspberries and blackberries

Fresh mint leaves

tools

18 by 13-inch baking sheet lined
with parchment paper

Piping bag fitted with an open star
tip of your choice

These crispy, sugary candied edible flowers are easy to make and add both prettiness and texture to a cake. They're also weirdly addictive, so don't be surprised if you find yourself snacking on them as if they were chips. You will want to make the candied flowers the night before so they have ample time to dry. I made this cake for my mom's birthday, with a crown of buttercream drop stars, fresh berries, candied flowers, and mint leaves. This would be very pretty for a spring tea party or bridal shower, too.

For an extra creamy tang, try the Whipped Cream Cheese Frosting (page 155) tinted in a pastel shade.

1. Make the candied flowers. The night before you plan to make the cake, very gently wash the flowers and petals and pat them dry with a clean paper towel. In a small bowl, mix together the meringue powder and water. Fill another small bowl with the superfine sugar. Handling the flowers and petals with a gentle touch, dunk one in the meringue powder mixture to coat completely. Remove it from the wet mixture and dip it into the sugar, turning it over to coat both sides. Place the coated flower or petal on the parchment-lined baking sheet. Continue this process until you have coated all of your flowers and petals. Let them dry completely overnight.

2. Prepare the cake. Bake the three layers of cake according to the recipe instructions. Level, fill, and frost your cake to the final coat stage (see page 6) using the vanilla buttercream.

3. Tint ½ cup of the remaining buttercream a light pink with the gel color and use it to fill the piping bag fitted with an open star tip. Reserve any leftover uncolored buttercream for later use.

4. Decorate the top of your frosted cake with a border crown of piped pink buttercream drop stars, candied petals and flowers, fresh berries, and fresh mint leaves. Finish with a craft paper flag if desired.

BUTTERCREAM FLOWER LETTER CAKE

for the cake base

Vegetable oil cooking spray

Parchment paper

1 rimmed 13 by 18 by 1-inch baking sheet

1 recipe cake of your choice (pages 146–48)

for the cake decoration

1½ recipes (about 7 to 8 cups) Simple Vanilla Buttercream (page 149) or 1¼ recipe (about 8 cups) Vanilla Swiss Meringue Buttercream (page 151)

¼ teaspoon gel food color in electric pink

¼ teaspoon gel food color in blue

¼ teaspoon gel food color in violet

¼ teaspoon gel food color in yellow

¼ teaspoon gel food color in leaf green

tools

Paper template of letter

Large rectangular cake board or decorative tray

5 piping bags fitted with various open star tips of your choice, including leaf tip

This is what happens when my love for clean typographical elements gets together with my love for buttercream flowers and they have a big old cake baby. I like the idea of making a whole name's worth of these (though you might want to avoid Rumpelstiltskin or anything else too long). These cakes would also be terribly cute as the initials of a wedded couple on a wedding cake table, to welcome a new baby at a baby shower, or with numbers for a birthday. Large, blocky letters and numerals work best for this cake, as you'll be cutting the shape out with a sharp paring knife. To create a template, you can freehand draw your chosen letter on a piece of letter paper or find something you like online and photocopy it, scaling it to fit onto a letter-sized sheet of paper. For larger letters, such as W or M, double the recipe and divide the batter evenly between two prepared rimmed baking sheets. Any leftover cake scraps make delicious snacks or can be saved for a layered trifle.

1. Prepare the cake. Using vegetable oil cooking spray, spray the rimmed baking sheet thoroughly. Place a piece of parchment paper cut to size on top and lightly spray again. Prepare the batter according to the recipe instructions. Pour the batter into the rimmed baking sheet and use an offset spatula to spread it to the edges in an even layer. Bake for 18 to 20 minutes, until a toothpick inserted into the center comes out clean and the cake is very lightly browned and springy to the touch.

2. Set the baking sheet on wire rack to cool. Immediately run an offset spatula around the edge of the cake to gently loosen the edges and prevent sticking or breaking. If the cake has puffed up a little bit, use a piece of parchment paper to very gently press it flat while the cake is still quite warm.

3. Put the cake in the freezer to power chill for 30 minutes. You don't want the cake to freeze, just to firm up to strengthen it for carving.

4. Remove the cake from the freezer. With the long side of the cake pan closest to you, look down on the cake and place the paper template you have made over the left half. Using a sharp paring knife, carefully cut out the letter. Place the template on the right half of the cake and repeat, positioning the letter upside down if you need to in order to make it fit. If the cake has warmed up, chill it again until it is firm, then proceed to cut out the second letter. Remove the scraps and save for snacking.

5. Freeze the tray with the letters for 15 minutes, until firm, making them easier to handle. Meanwhile, have a rectangular cake board or decorative tray ready.

6. Once the letters are firm again, use your hands to carefully but deftly place the first letter onto the cake board. Using an offset spatula, spread a generous layer of buttercream on top. Carefully but swiftly position the cold and firm second letter on top of the first, gently pressing down to adhere it to the buttercream. Crumb coat the entire cake with buttercream (see page 4), evening out the edges with a cake bench scraper until you are happy with the smoothness of your frosting job.

7. Divide the remaining buttercream into five small bowls, tinting each bowl of frosting with your choice of gel coloring.

8. Fill your piping bags fitted with various open star tips with the different shades of buttercream. Save the leaf tip piping bag for the green buttercream.

9. Pipe drop stars, rosettes, and leaves all over the cake (see pages 7–8).

TIP If you have a cutout shape in your letter, such as the hole in the letter A or R, freeze the cake to firm up after you've piped all of the buttercream. Once it's frozen, use a sharp, clean paring knife to trim the buttercream off the letter hole, making the letter more recognizable.

BASIC RECIPES

VANILLA CREAM CAKE

I love this not-too-sweet vanilla butter cake. It uses cake flour, but gets a sturdier-crumb boost from 4 large eggs and 1 cup of heavy cream. Frost it with Simple Vanilla Buttercream and rainbow sprinkles, and you'll be whisked through space and time back to a heavenly childhood dream.

Makes three 8 by 2-inch round cake layers or around 28 regular-size cupcakes (cupcake liners filled two-thirds full)

1 cup unsalted butter, room temperature

1¾ cups granulated white sugar

4 large eggs

2 teaspoons pure vanilla extract

3 cups cake flour

1 tablespoon baking powder

½ teaspoon salt

1 cup heavy cream

1 cup whole milk

Preheat the oven to 350°F. Prepare three 8 by 2-inch round cake pans as described on page 1.

In the bowl of a stand mixer fitted with the paddle attachment, beat the butter and sugar on high speed until light and fluffy, about 2 minutes, scraping down the sides of the bowl with a spatula as needed. Turn the mixer down to low speed and add the eggs one at a time until incorporated, then add the vanilla extract.

In a large bowl, use a balloon whisk to mix together the flour, baking powder, and salt.

In a large liquid measuring cup, whisk together the cream and the milk.

With the mixer on low speed, add one-third of the flour mixture, then half of the milk mixture. Keep alternating as you add the mixtures, finishing with the dry ingredients. I mix for about 30 to 60 seconds total—you do not want to overmix this batter, but be sure the ingredients are incorporated.

Divide the batter evenly among the prepared cake pans and smooth the tops with an offset spatula. Bake for 20 to 25 minutes, checking for doneness at 20 minutes. The cakes will be done when a toothpick inserted in the centers comes out clean and the tops of the cakes are light golden brown.

Cool the cakes completely in their pans before frosting. Or, alternatively, cool them for 30 minutes in their pans and then gently turn them out onto a wire rack to finish cooling completely.

ONE BOWL DARK CHOCOLATE CAKE

This is my favorite chocolate cake recipe for many reasons: its deep chocolate flavor, its tender crumb, and its easiness factor. I make my own buttermilk substitute for this cake, using whole milk and vinegar. The batter is sneakily on the liquidy side, but don't be alarmed. It will bake into a beautifully moist, springy, chocolaty cake. This recipe is adapted from Ina Garten's recipe "Beatty's Chocolate Cake."

Makes three 8 by 2-inch round cake layers or around 28 regular-size cupcakes (cupcake liners filled two-thirds full)

1 cup whole milk

1 teaspoon white vinegar

1¾ cups unbleached all-purpose flour

2 cups granulated white sugar

1 cup good-quality Dutch-processed cocoa powder

2 teaspoons baking soda

1 teaspoon baking powder

1 teaspoon kosher salt

½ cup vegetable oil

2 large eggs, room temperature

2 teaspoons pure vanilla extract

1 cup freshly brewed hot coffee (I use 2 shots of freshly brewed espresso topped up with hot water to equal 1 cup)

Preheat the oven to 350°F. Prepare three 8 by 2-inch round cake pans as described on page 1.

In a liquid measuring cup, mix together the whole milk and the white vinegar. Let the mixture sit until curdled, about 10 minutes.

In the meantime, in the bowl of a stand mixer fitted with the paddle attachment, mix together on low speed the flour, sugar, cocoa powder, baking soda, baking powder, and salt.

Once the milk is curdled, whisk it in a large bowl with the vegetable oil, eggs, and vanilla extract until combined.

With the mixer on low speed, slowly pour the wet mixture into the dry mixture. Add the hot coffee and mix just until the batter is incorporated, about 30 seconds.

Divide the batter among the prepared cake pans and smooth the tops with an offset spatula. Bake for 20 to 25 minutes, checking for doneness at 20 minutes. The cakes will be done when a toothpick inserted in the centers comes out clean and the cakes are springy to the touch.

Cool the cakes completely in their pans before frosting. Or, alternatively, cool them for 30 minutes in their pans and then gently turn them out onto a wire rack to finish cooling completely.

VEGAN CHOCOLATE CAKE

This cake is very chocolaty; the full-fat coconut milk makes it rich and moist. The crumb is slightly more delicate than that of a cake made with eggs, so chill the layers before frosting to avoid any tearing of the cake, and frost it gently, as if you are petting a newborn kitten.

Makes three 8 by 2-inch round cake layers or around 28 regular-size cupcakes (cupcake liners filled two-thirds full)

2½ cups unbleached all-purpose flour

1½ cups good-quality Dutch-processed cocoa powder

2 cups granulated white sugar

2½ teaspoons baking soda

1¼ teaspoons baking powder

1¼ teaspoons kosher salt

Egg replacer equivalent to 3 eggs (see Note below)

2¼ cups full-fat coconut milk

½ cup plus 2 tablespoons vegetable oil

2 teaspoons pure vanilla extract

TIP If the cake layers bake up with domes, you can very gently and carefully flatten the domes with your hands on top of a piece of parchment paper until level while the cake is still quite warm. Or you can wait until they are completely cool and use a serrated bread knife to level the layers (see page 5).

Set the oven rack in the middle and preheat the oven to 350°F. Prepare three 8 by 2-inch round cake pans as described on page 1.

In the bowl of a stand mixer fitted with the paddle attachment, mix together the flour, cocoa powder, sugar, baking soda, baking powder, and salt on low speed until combined. Prepare the egg replacer according to the box instructions. With the mixer turned off, add the egg replacer mix, coconut milk, vegetable oil, and vanilla extract. Turn the mixer on to the lowest speed and mix just to combine, about 1 minute. Do not overmix.

Divide the batter evenly among the three prepared cake pans and bake for 20 to 25 minutes, turning the pans halfway through the process to ensure even baking and checking after around 20 minutes for doneness. Cakes are finished when a cake tester or wooden toothpick inserted in the middle comes out clean and the cakes spring back when touched lightly and delicately (they will be hot!).

Cool the cakes completely in their pans before frosting.

Note: I use egg replacer purchased at a store; it is a mixture of cornstarch, potato starch, soy flour, baking powder, and guar gum. You could also use 2 ripe, mashed bananas. Egg replacer helps thicken the cake batter and gives some sturdiness to the finished product. Look for egg replacer online or at your local health food store.

SIMPLE VANILLA BUTTERCREAM

I find that most of the time, American-style buttercream can be too sweet. My Simple Vanilla Buttercream is very simple indeed: unsalted butter, confectioner's' sugar, pure vanilla extract, and a dash of milk, if needed. The ratio of butter to sugar, however, is much more sane than your typical recipe and produces a buttercream that is much less sweet. Don't skip the sifting step—it's essential to prevent any clumps or clogged piping tips. This is a perfect buttercream that frosts and pipes easily for all your cake decorating and birthday party needs.

Makes about 4 to 5 cups

2 cups unsalted butter, room temperature

4 cups confectioners' sugar, sifted

2 teaspoons pure vanilla extract

1 to 2 teaspoons whole milk, optional. If the buttercream is too stiff, a touch of milk will help loosen it a little.

In the bowl of a stand mixer with a paddle attachment, beat the butter on high speed until it is light and fluffy, about 2 minutes. Scrape down the sides of the bowl with a spatula. Add the sifted confectioners' sugar, vanilla extract, and milk, if using. Mix on low speed to combine the ingredients. Once the sugar is incorporated, crank the mixer to high speed and beat the mixture for another 2 minutes, until it has more than doubled in volume, for a fluffy whipped frosting.

Leftover buttercream can be stored in an airtight container in the fridge for up to 2 weeks or in the freezer for 1 month; bring it back to room temperature and rewhip in a stand mixer before using. This recipe can easily be halved or doubled.

SIMPLE CHOCOLATE BUTTERCREAM

Another easy, not too sweet buttercream recipe, this simple chocolate buttercream is a cinch to whip together and is less sweet than a fudge frosting made with melted chocolate. This buttercream darkens in color over time, giving it a rich chocolate appearance.

Makes about 5 cups

2 cups unsalted butter, room temperature

3 cups confectioners' sugar, sifted

1 cup good-quality Dutch-processed cocoa powder, sifted

2 teaspoons pure vanilla extract

Pinch of salt

1 to 2 teaspoons whole milk, optional. If the buttercream is too stiff, a touch of milk will help loosen it a little.

In the bowl of a stand mixer fitted with the paddle attachment, beat the butter on high speed for 2 minutes. Scrape down the sides of the bowl with a spatula. With the mixer off, carefully add the sifted confectioners' sugar, sifted cocoa powder, vanilla extract, salt, and milk, if using. Here is a trick for preventing a fine dusting of cocoa powder from settling all over your kitchen: cover the mixer tightly with a large, damp tea towel or, if your mixing bowl has a cover, use that. Turn the mixer on low speed to incorporate ingredients, then beat the mixture on high speed for 2 minutes, until it has more than doubled in volume and a light, fluffy chocolate buttercream has formed.

Leftover buttercream can be stored in an airtight container in the fridge for up to 2 weeks or in the freezer for 1 month; bring it back to room temperature and rewhip in a stand mixer before using. This recipe can easily be halved or doubled.

Note: If your buttercream feels too stiff for frosting or piping, add ¼ cup more unsalted butter and/or 1 teaspoon of milk, beat on low speed to incorporate, then beat on high speed to fluff up.

VANILLA SWISS MERINGUE BUTTERCREAM

People say that Swiss meringue buttercream is "too buttery" and sometimes tastes like whipped butter. I fiddled for a long time with the sugar-to-butter ratio for this buttercream. It's not a standard ratio, but it's my favorite iteration, producing a frosting that is silky, creamy, sweet, and buttery, like dreamy vanilla ice cream. Crack and separate fresh eggs for this. You can store the unused yolks in the freezer—mix each yolk with ½ teaspoon of sugar—for future use in ice cream or custard recipes.

Makes about 6 cups

1 cup egg whites (about 7 to 8 large eggs)

2¼ cups granulated white sugar

2½ cups unsalted butter, room temperature, cut into 1-inch cubes

2 teaspoons pure vanilla extract

Seeds of 1 vanilla bean (optional)

Pinch of fine sea salt

Gel color of choice, if using

To ensure that the metal bowl of your stand mixer is completely clean, dry, and free of grease, give it a quick wipe out with a halved lemon, then rinse and dry it thoroughly.

In the bowl of a stand mixer fitted with the whisk attachment, mix the egg whites and the sugar on low to combine into a sugary slurry. Fill a medium saucepan with a few inches of water and place it on the stovetop over medium-high heat. Set the mixer bowl on top of the saucepan to create a kind of double boiler, making sure the mixer bowl doesn't touch the water.

Heat the egg and sugar mixture until it reaches 160°F on a thermometer or is hot to the touch, whisking occasionally. This usually takes about 5 to 7 minutes.

Carefully return the metal mixing bowl to the stand mixer, with the whisk attachment in place. Now, bring the mixer up to high speed and beat the mixture for 8 to 10 minutes, until you've created medium-stiff peaks and it's a billowy, sticky, cloudy meringue. Whipping the meringue will also help cool down the bowl.

Swap out the whisk for the paddle attachment. Make sure your meringue has cooled sufficiently before adding the butter—the bowl shouldn't be hot, just slightly warm, if that. With the mixer on low speed, add the butter a few pieces at a time, until all the butter is incorporated—it will look like a thick soup at this point. Add the vanilla extract,

Strawberry Swiss Meringue Buttercream. Omit the vanilla extract. Make a strawberry purée by blending 1 pint washed and hulled fresh strawberries, ⅛ cup sugar, and a pinch of salt in a blender. Add 1 cup purée (or use puréed double fruit strawberry jam) and 2 tablespoons freeze-dried strawberry powder to the buttercream after the butter has been added. (Blitz freeze-dried strawberries in a food processor until they become a fine powder.) To make the frosting more pink, add ⅛ teaspoon pink gel color.

Caramel Swiss Meringue Buttercream. Omit the vanilla extract and add 1 cup cara-mel after the butter has been added (either homemade or store-bought caramel in a jar).

Coffee Swiss Meringue Buttercream. Omit the vanilla extract and substitute 1 tablespoon pure coffee extract after the butter has been added.

the vanilla bean seeds, if using, along with the pinch of salt (and any small amount of gel color if so desired), then bring the speed up to medium-high and beat until a fluffy, silky, magical buttercream has formed, about 2 to 3 minutes.

Vanilla Swiss Meringue Buttercream will keep in an airtight container for up to 1 week in the fridge or up to 1 month in the freezer. Bring it back to room temperature and gently rewhip before using.

TIPS If your Swiss meringue buttercream turns into a soupy disaster, try placing the whole bowl in the fridge for about 5 to 10 minutes to cool it down a bit, then bring it out and try whipping it again, first on low speed, then bringing it up to high speed. Or try adding a few more pieces of butter to the mix.

If your Swiss meringue buttercream becomes a gross-looking, curdled mess, try lightly heating the whole bowl over a low-boiling pot of water for 1 minute, just to get some heat back in there. Once it's warmed up a teensy bit, try mixing it again. You will be amazed at how a bowl of seemingly awful-looking buttercream can actually be saved and whipped back into a gorgeous, fluffy, satiny, creamy frosting.

VEGAN CHOCOLATE WHIPPED GANACHE FROSTING

This is my favorite frosting to use for any vegan cake or cupcake. It will thicken as it cools and can then be whipped into a spreadable frosting. Rich, decadent, and a win for both vegans and their nonvegan friends!

Paired with the Vegan Choclate Cake, this recipe would make an excellent vegan brown dog cake (page 29 or 53) or bear cake (page 17)—simply use vegan fondant for facial features. To have enough frosting for filling, covering, and piping an entire cake, double the recipe.

Makes about 3½ cups

2 cups full-fat coconut milk

1 pound best-quality dairy-free chocolate, finely chopped

In a medium saucepan over medium-high heat, bring the coconut milk to a low boil, keeping an eye on it to ensure it doesn't burn. Remove the pan from the heat and add the chocolate, swirling the pan so the hot coconut milk covers the chocolate completely. Let the mixture stand untouched for 10 minutes. Slowly whisk the mixture until a shiny, smooth ganache comes together before your eyes.

Power chill the ganache in the freezer for 20 to 25 minutes. The ganache will thicken as it cools, but keep your eye on it to ensure it doesn't actually freeze. Once it has cooled and thickened to a spreadable consistency, transfer the mixture to the bowl of your stand mixer fitted with the paddle attachment. Beat on high until light and fluffy, about 2 to 3 minutes. Use immediately to fill and frost your cake.

Ganache will keep for up to 1 week in the fridge and will solidify when refrigerated. Bring it back to room temperature and gently rewhip before using.

CHOCOLATE GANACHE DRIP

The cake drip has been experiencing a moment in the cake decorating world, and for good reason—I love its artful, painterly style. It's simple to make, too. You can substitute high-quality semisweet chocolate chips for the finely chopped chocolate, if you like.

Makes about 1½ cups

1 cup heavy cream

2 cups best-quality semisweet chocolate, finely chopped

In a small saucepan over medium-high heat, bring the heavy cream to a low boil, keeping an eye on it to ensure it doesn't burn. Remove the pan from the heat and add the chocolate, swirling the pan so the cream covers the chocolate. Let the mixture stand untouched for 10 minutes. Slowly whisk the mixture until a shiny, smooth ganache comes together before your eyes.

The ganache will thicken as it cools. Before dripping it onto your cake, make sure the ganache is cool but still dripable. Use a spoon to test the consistency before applying it to your cake. To cool the ganache quickly, power chill it in the freezer for 15 to 20 minutes, keeping an eye on it to ensure it doesn't get too thick.

This ganache keeps for up to 1 week in the fridge. To bring it back to dripping consistency, heat it up gently over low heat on the stove or in seconds-long zaps in the microwave.

WHIPPED CREAM CHEESE FROSTING

Cream cheese frosting is a bit of a weakness of mine, especially when slathered on layers of carrot cake. Back when I had my cake business, I would use this rich, tangy frosting to top chocolate cupcakes (I named it Brown Velour, a cousin to Red Velvet) and the combination was a best seller. This is a simple vanilla cream cheese frosting, which can be used to pipe animal fur as well, but if you find it a little looser, add more confectioners' sugar, ⅛ cup at a time.

Makes 4 cups

One 8-ounce (250-gram) package cream cheese, room temperature

1 cup unsalted butter, room temperature

4 cups confectioners' sugar, sifted

2 teaspoons pure vanilla extract

In the bowl of a stand mixer fitted with the paddle attachment, beat the cream cheese and butter together on high speed until light and fluffy, about 2 minutes. With the mixer on low speed, add the sifted confectioners' sugar ½ cup at a time and beat until incorporated. Add the vanilla extract, then beat again on high speed for another few minutes, until the mixture is fully whipped and has doubled in volume.

Cream cheese frosting will keep for up to 1 week in the fridge. Bring it back to room temperature and rewhip before using.

PEANUT BUTTER FROSTING

This is not the time for your fancy organic all-natural peanut butter. This is the time for your supermarket jar of smooth and creamy PB, the kind that contains sugar and that you dip your giant spoon into when you need to engage in emotional eating. This recipe can be made vegan by swapping out the butter for a vegan butter product, such as Earth Balance natural shortening sticks, for the butter.

Makes 4 to 5 cups

2½ cups unsalted butter, room temperature

1½ cups creamy peanut butter

3 cups confectioners' sugar, sifted

2 teaspoons pure vanilla extract

In the bowl of a stand mixer fitted with the paddle attachment, beat the butter and peanut butter on high speed for 1 minute. Scrape down the sides of the bowl with a spatula, then add the sifted confectioners' sugar and vanilla extract. Beat the mixture until it is light and fluffy, about 2 to 3 minutes.

Peanut Butter Frosting will keep in an airtight container in the fridge for up to 1 week. Bring it back to room temperature and rewhip before using.

SWISS MERINGUE KISSES

These crispy, chewy meringues are your cake-topping friends—they are like airy, crispy bites of cotton candy. Crush them to make sprinkles and to add texture, place them on top of your cake with piped buttercream or edible flowers, or package them up for holiday gifting. This recipe makes perfectly pipable, thick, and glossy meringue kisses. Color the meringue and use it to fill a piping bag fitted with an open star tip or use an open circle tip for the classic "kiss" look.

Makes approximately
a hundred 1-inch kisses

4 large egg whites

¾ cup granulated sugar

⅛ teaspoon gel food color in color of your choice

TIP When decorating a buttercream cake, place the meringue kisses on the cake no more than 1 hour before serving, so that the moisture from the buttercream doesn't soften the meringues.

Preheat the oven to 180°F. Line three baking sheets with parchment paper.

In the metal bowl of a stand mixer fitted with the whisk attachment, mix the egg whites and sugar to combine. Place the bowl on top of a medium-size pot filled with a few inches of water, effectively creating a double boiler. Over medium-high heat, whisk the mixture intermittently until the temperature reaches 160°F on a thermometer, or is hot to the touch, and the sugar crystals have dissolved.

Carefully transfer the metal bowl back to the stand mixer fitted with the whisk attachment. Whisk the mixture on medium speed for 2 to 3 minutes, then raise to high speed for 7 to 8 minutes, until the meringue becomes white, fluffy, and glossy and it holds stiff peaks.

Gently fold in the gel food color of your choice or divide the meringue into bowls and tint individually with different colors.

Fill a piping bag fitted with an open circle or open star tip with meringue. Pipe 1-inch meringue kisses on the parchment paper–covered baking sheets. Bake for 1 hour in the oven. Turn off the oven and let the kisses dry out for another hour. If they still seem sticky, leave them in the oven with the oven turned off for 2 to 3 hours more, but be careful they don't end up browning.

Store the meringue kisses in an airtight container for up to 1 week. If they get soft, crisp them up in the oven at 180°F for about 15 minutes, then let them cool before use.

TEMPLATES

BLUE BEAR CAKE
Paper Party Garland (page 19)

BROWN CURLY-HAIRED PUP CAKE
Happy Birthday Bone (page 55)

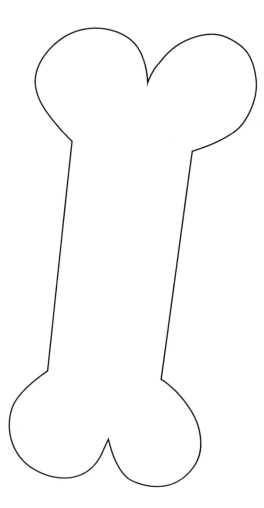

VINTAGE SAILBOAT CAKE
Sailboat and Moon (page 65)

STRAWBERRY CAKE
Strawberry Stem (page 77)

KAWAII PINEAPPLE CAKE
Pineapple Wearing Sunglasses and Speech Bubble (page 73)

KAWAII PINEAPPLE CAKE
Pineapple Stem (page 73)

please print at 200%

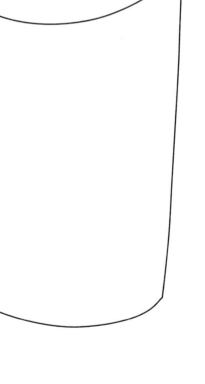

BURGER CAKE
Soda and Fries Toppers (page 81)

RES●URCES

EQUIPMENT

Fat Daddio's I use their cake pans in a bunch of different sizes—they do the job! fatdaddios.com.

KitchenAid For heavy-duty stand mixers that will last a lifetime. kitchenaid.com.

Scoop n Save The Canadian spot for all cake-related items—piping bags, piping tips, cake boards, et cetera! scoop-n-save.com.

Wilton Enterprises Wilton is known for cake-decorating supplies—piping tips galore, meringue powder, and so much more. They make the sports ball cake pan, which I like using for a myriad of applications. wilton.com.

Amazon I try to shop local, but oftentimes Amazon comes to the rescue. For alphabet letter stamps, cake supplies, candy melts, white chocolate, gel food color, silicone alphabet letter molds, cake boards—pretty much everything. amazon.com.

INGREDIENTS

AmeriColor Corp. I love their gel colors, and the Gourmet Writer pens are fun, too! americolorcorp.com.

India Tree Go au naturel with their all-natural gel food colors and sprinkles, too. They also carry white sugar pearls. indiatree.com.

Rodelle Kitchen For high-quality cocoa powder and pure vanilla extracts. rodellekitchen.com.

Sugarfina For fancy candies. sugarfina.com.

Sweetapolita For the cutest sprinkle mixes anywhere. sweetapolitashop.com.

Wilton Enterprises wilton.com.

CRAFT SUPPLIES

Cu-te-ta-pe For baker's twine and washi tape. cutetape.com.

Meri Meri For alphabet stickers. merimeri.com.

Michael's For craft punches, craft paper, letter stickers, and a range of other craft supplies. michaels.com.

DECORATIONS

Hip! Hip! For supercute cake toppers, letter balloons, and well-designed party ware. hiphip.co.

Meri Meri merimeri.com.

My Little Day For incredibly adorable party ware—cups, plates, decor, et cetera. mylittleday.fr.

HOUSEWARES

Food52 For an array of modern, stylish kitchenware. food52.com/shop.

Herriott Grace For beautiful ceramics and styling supplies. herriottgrace.com.

Imm Living For fun cake stands. imm-living.com.

For home ware/food styling–type stuff, I love supporting indie and local ceramic artists. Garage sales, antique sales, and thrift stores are awesome for finding vintage flatware and other treasures, too.

ACKNOWLEDGMENTS

I know my book writing process was quite different than many others—shortly after my book deal, I was diagnosed with breast cancer, and my book production was put on hold for two years. I was fearful of so many things, including losing my book deal that I had dreamt of my whole life, as well as not being sure I would have the energy and creative drive to work through and finish it. I would like to express my huge thanks and gratitude to the wonderful team at Roost Books—Sara, Jenn, Jess, Audra, Liz, and Daniel. Jenn—I have felt truly cared for and supported in this process and I feel lucky to have gotten to work with you. In times of self-doubt, you were always encouraging, positive, and constructive. Sara—I respect and admire the creative empire that you are building, and feel completely fortunate to be a part of the Roost community of authors. Audra—thank you for your eagle eye; copy editing ain't no joke! Stokeage level high! Liz, I can't thank you enough for the beautiful design. It feels so true to the vibe of *Coco Cake Land* and I love it!

To my agent, Brandi—thank you for believing in my blog and writing, and for helping me achieve my dream of becoming a published author.

To my husband, Rich—a teensy paragraph is no use in expressing how much I love you, and how much your love and support mean to me. The squalls have been wild, but the fair winds have been sweet and aplenty. Thank you for the countless times in which you've talked me off a ledge of doubt, and for always believing in me and for making me laugh. I love you more than a fit-and-fat Chinese Pumpkin loves cake. Thank you for everything you do for me and Teddy!

To my son, Teddy—having you changed my life completely. You bring huge joy, laughter, and complexity to my life, and our little family makes me so happy. Continue to be strong but sweet, compassionate and thoughtful, loving and respectful. Never stop learning. I am so proud of you and the little person you are becoming.

To my amazing mom and dad—you always knew I was a nut, yet you have supported me through decades of "careers," creative impulses, and delightful phases. Thank you for teaching me how to be a caring and good person in this world, and for showing me that family, friends, love, and the relationships we cultivate mean the most out of everything. Dad, thank you for "liking" every Instagram post and for your occasional but hilariously "Gerry Sung" comments on my blog. Mom, thank you for being an example of a strong woman, wonderful mother, and the best grandma to all the kids. I love you both more than words can say!

To my Sung Sisters, Leanne and Shelley—I love you guys! You have supported me through thick and thin, and are the number one champions of *Coco Cake Land*. Thank you for being my best friends and the best sisters one could ever have! To my nieces and nephews, I love you guys!

To my mother-in-law, Beth, and my late father-in-law, Aleck—I won the in-law lottery. Thank you for loving your Chinese daughter!

To my late Poh-poh—I miss you and wish you were around to flip through the pages of my book. Thank you for inspiring me to bake and cook.

To my Auntie Cor—having you in my life is very special to me. Thank you for all of your love, kindness, and support!

To my extended family, in-laws, and especially my wonderful aunties and beloved cousins—there are few extended families as close as we are. Your support through all the hard stuff and the good stuff, I won't ever forget.

To my amazing friends! Hashtag blessed one million times over. I'm crazily lucky to count so many caring people as friends. Thanks to the incredible group of people I know and love: Tara, Christa, Erika, Toni, Sharon, Amber, Shira, Becky, Amy, Jamie, Ashley, Heather, Miko, Sarah VS, Lori, Kaleb, Helen, Erin B., and countless others. Thank you also to Cor for taking such good care of Teddy while I worked on this book.

To my beautiful blog friends—especially Steph and Tessa—thank you for the hangouts, deep vault sessions, snacks, and laughs. Big love and thanks to my other faves, Jan, Cynthia, Michelle, Alana, and Molly. To the finest women ever of *Cherry Bombe* magazine—thank you for existing, for your support of me, and for being endless champions of the huge diversity of voices of women in food!

Thank you to Rachel and her blog *Handmade Charlotte,* where my fox cake, lamb cake, and strawberry cake first had their debut.

To all the incredible people I've met both online and in real life through this wild and wacky blogging community—thank you for being friends, fans, supporters, and readers of my blog. To the early supporters and clients of my cakes and cake designs, thank you for the positive encouragement and support!

Finally, thank you to my grade 4 teacher, Mrs. Laurel Gurnsey. When I was nine years old, I wrote a super-goth and maybe a little violent but visually descriptive story about a rare and beautiful Pegasus being murdered by crystal elves under the order of King Labreska. Thank you for saving this story, giving it to me thirty years later, and being my very favorite teacher, who encouraged me so positively and strongly to pursue writing.

INDEX

ABOUT THE AUTHOR

LORI KIESSLING

LYNDSAY SUNG is the self-taught baker, blogger, and mama behind the blog *Coco Cake Land* (cococakeland .com), a site filled with colorful cakes, vibrant photography, and plenty of jokes. Lyndsay lives and works in Vancouver, British Columbia, with her husband, Rich, and their son, Teddy.